W9-BEU-057

WEEKEND
ROUTING PROJECTS

Easy step-by-step designs
in light and dark wood

ANDY STANDING

NEW HOLLAND

Published in 2006 by
New Holland Publishers (UK) Ltd
London · Cape Town · Sydney · Auckland
www.newhollandpublishers.com

Garfield House, 86–88 Edgware Road, London W2 2EA, United Kingdom

80 McKenzie Street, Cape Town 8001, South Africa
Level 1, Unit 4, 14 Aquatic Drive, Frenchs Forest, NSW 2086, Australia
218 Lake Road, Northcote, Auckland, New Zealand

ISBN 1 84537 281 6

Senior Editor: Clare Sayer
Production: Hazel Kirkman
Design: Alan Marshall
Project photography: Edward Allwright
Step-by-step photography: Andy Standing
Editorial Direction: Rosemary Wilkinson

1 3 5 7 9 10 8 6 4 2

Reproduction by Modern Age Repro House Ltd, Hong Kong
Printed and bound by Times Offset (M) Sdn Bhd, Malaysia

The information in this book is true and complete to the best of our knowledge. All recommendations
are made without guarantee on the part of the author and the publishers. The author and publishers
disclaim any liability for damages or injury resulting from the use of this information.

Contents

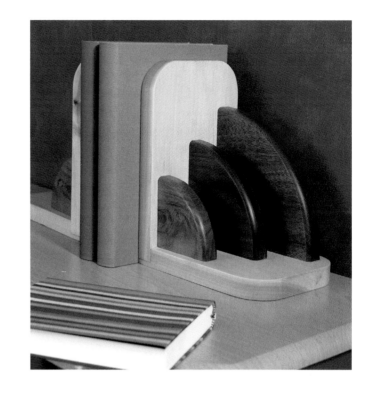

Introduction

I have been involved in woodworking for many years and have always been a keen user of power tools and machinery. One of my favourite and most-used tools is the router – at the last count I had six of them in my workshop! This book is intended to give both the novice and more experienced user an insight into the workings and uses of this amazing machine. I have tried to keep the design of the projects simple, while at the same time retaining a professional look. All too often the projects in the simpler woodworking books look so homemade that you are not really inspired to make them. I hope that is not the case here. I have supplied plan drawings with every project so it would be a fairly straightforward task to adjust the dimensions of the plans to suit your particular needs, though try to keep the proportions the same. Feel free to experiment with different timbers too, but remember to buy the best quality that you can afford, as it will greatly improve the finished piece. You will, of course, need other tools apart from the router but many of these will be part of your basic woodworking tool kit. A section at the beginning of the book details all this and more.

Finally, I hope that you enjoy making the pieces and are proud of the results. Perhaps, when you have finished the book you will feel confident enough to work on more challenging projects – or maybe even start designing your own!

Andy Standing

Beginner's guide to routing

Routers are incredibly versatile tools, which are capable of undertaking a wide range of woodworking jobs. However, they can appear to be mysterious and intimidating machines. This chapter will help you to understand how the tool works and learn how to use it safely and effectively.

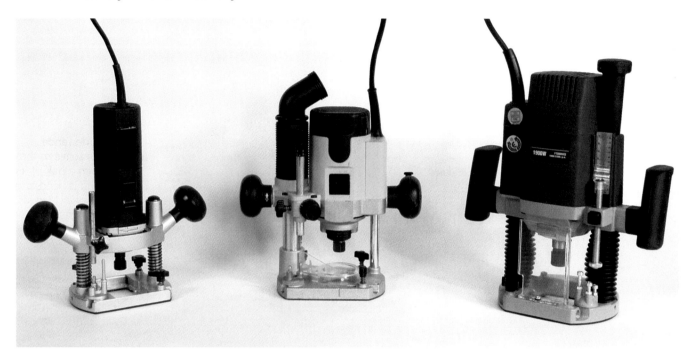

USING A ROUTER SAFELY

Routers can be dangerous, so follow these basic safety precautions.
• Always disconnect the machine from the power supply before changing cutters.
• Check all settings, and make sure that everything is tightened before starting work.
• The workpiece must be securely clamped to the bench before you start.
• Use a dust extractor and wear safety glasses, ear defenders and a dust mask.
• Make several shallow cuts rather than one deep one. Never make a cut deeper than the diameter of the cutter you are using in one pass. For example, to make a groove 8 mm (5/16 in) deep, make two passes each 3 mm (1/8 in) deep, followed by a 2-mm (1/16-in) pass. This puts less strain on the machine.

Routers are produced in a range of different sizes. The smallest, shown on the left, is easy to handle and economical to buy, though only powerful enough to cope with light jobs. The mid-sized model in the centre is a versatile machine with a more powerful motor and sophisticated features, suitable for more sustained use. The machine on the right is a heavyweight tool with a 12-mm (½-in) collet. It can cope with most jobs and is powerful enough to drive the largest cutters.

First steps
The key to safe woodworking is an understanding of the tools that are used, so before you go any further, examine your router and learn what all the parts are, and how they operate.
The machine itself is made in two main parts: the body and the base. See opposite for information on the main components and their functions.

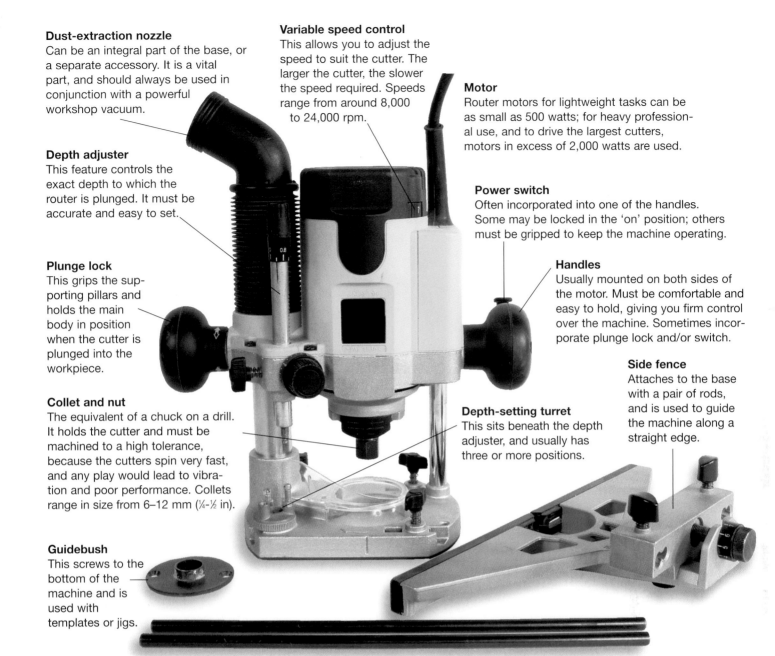

Dust-extraction nozzle
Can be an integral part of the base, or a separate accessory. It is a vital part, and should always be used in conjunction with a powerful workshop vacuum.

Depth adjuster
This feature controls the exact depth to which the router is plunged. It must be accurate and easy to set.

Plunge lock
This grips the supporting pillars and holds the main body in position when the cutter is plunged into the workpiece.

Collet and nut
The equivalent of a chuck on a drill. It holds the cutter and must be machined to a high tolerance, because the cutters spin very fast, and any play would lead to vibration and poor performance. Collets range in size from 6–12 mm (¼-½ in).

Guidebush
This screws to the bottom of the machine and is used with templates or jigs.

Variable speed control
This allows you to adjust the speed to suit the cutter. The larger the cutter, the slower the speed required. Speeds range from around 8,000 to 24,000 rpm.

Motor
Router motors for lightweight tasks can be as small as 500 watts; for heavy professional use, and to drive the largest cutters, motors in excess of 2,000 watts are used.

Power switch
Often incorporated into one of the handles. Some may be locked in the 'on' position; others must be gripped to keep the machine operating.

Handles
Usually mounted on both sides of the motor. Must be comfortable and easy to hold, giving you firm control over the machine. Sometimes incorporate plunge lock and/or switch.

Side fence
Attaches to the base with a pair of rods, and is used to guide the machine along a straight edge.

Depth-setting turret
This sits beneath the depth adjuster, and usually has three or more positions.

Router cutters

It is important to understand how the cutter operates and how the direction of rotation governs performance. The cutter rotates in a clockwise direction when viewed from above. This means that if you plunge the cutter into a workpiece and push the router away from you, it will pull to the left. Therefore, when pushing the router, the side fence must be mounted on the right, as shown. If you prefer to pull the router towards you, the fence must be on the left. When using a bearing-guided cutter (see page 12) on the edge of a workpiece, you must go round it in an anticlockwise direction; however when moulding an internal edge, such as a frame, move in a clockwise direction. This means that you are feeding the work against the direction of bit rotation, making the machine bite into the timber and push back against the operator. If you try to reverse these directions, the machine will be pulling away from you all the time. This makes the router dangerous and difficult to control, particularly if using large-diameter cutters.

First cuts

If you are new to routing it is very important to familiarize yourself with the way the router works. Before you start work on any project, practise on some off-cuts of timber so that you avoid spoiling and wasting expensive pieces of timber.

For your first attempt at routing, choose a simple task such as cutting a straight groove in a piece of softwood. Follow the steps below and take your time – before long you will be routing with confidence.

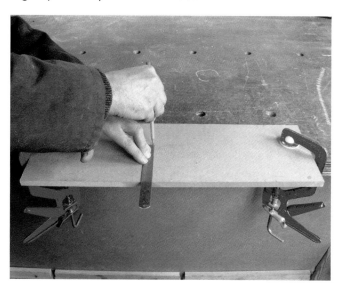

1 Clamp the workpiece firmly to the workbench, with its edge just overhanging the front. Draw a short pencil line parallel to the short edge and about 100 mm (4 in) in.

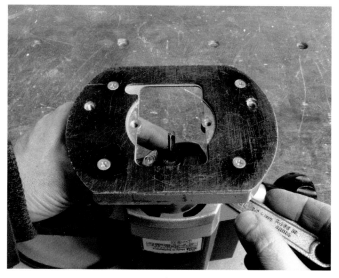

2 With the power disconnected, stand the router upside down on the workbench and insert a straight cutter, 6 mm (¼ in) in diameter. Make sure that at least three-quarters of the cutter shank is in the collet. Tighten securely with a spanner.

3 With the router upright, loosely fit the side fence to the right-hand side.

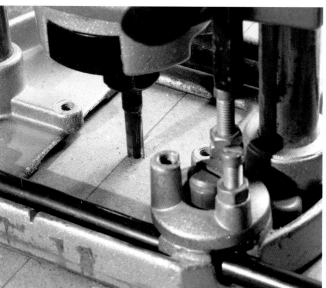

4 Stand the disconnected router on the workpiece and plunge the bit so that it just touches the surface. Engage the plunge lock. Place the bit on the marked line and adjust the fence so that it is tight against the edge.

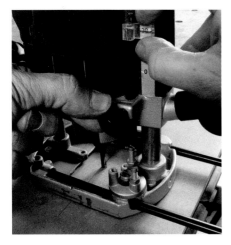

5 To set the cutting depth, leave the cutter touching the surface and wind the depth adjusting rod down so that it touches the turret. If possible, zero the scale and then wind the rod back the desired amount, which in this case is 4 mm (³⁄₁₆ in). Lock the rod in place and release the plunge lock so that the router returns to the top of its travel.

6 You are now ready to make the cut. Before you do so, set the variable speed control to maximum (because you are using a small-diameter cutter), and check that all the adjustment screws are tight on the fence and depth adjuster. Connect the power and dust extractor.

7 Position the router at the beginning of the cut. Make sure that the fence is tight against the side of the workpiece. Grip the handles and start the motor. When it is up to full speed, plunge the cutter into the workpiece and engage the plunge lock. Push the router forward, making sure that the side fence is still against the edge. It will now cut a straight groove.

Working at the right speed

Make sure that you move the tool at the optimum speed. If you move too slowly, the bit will overheat and there will be burn marks on the workpiece; too fast and the motor will strain and the cutting process will be difficult. With practice, you will soon get a feel for it. When you reach the end of the cut, release the plunge lock and let the cutter rise out of the workpiece. Turn off the motor and, once it has stopped, put the router aside.

Removing a cutter

To release the cutter the collet must be pulled out of the central shaft by the collet nut. This means that the collet nut effectively has to be loosened twice. Initial loosening releases the pressure on the lower shoulder of the collet, and the nut may be turned by hand. The collet remains held in the shaft, so the cutter cannot be removed. As the nut is loosened, it begins to get stiff again as it contacts the upper shoulder of the collet. A spanner is now needed: this time the nut will pull the collet from the tapered shaft, and it will then release its grip on the bit.

Checklist

Routing may look a little complicated, but that isn't the case as long as you follow these simple rules:
• Make sure the workpiece is securely fixed before you start. Position any clamps so that they will not interfere with the router's movement.
• Make several shallow cuts rather than one deep one.
• Use the variable speed function to suit the cutter and feed rate. Large cutters need slower speeds.
• Plan your work carefully. Have a 'dry run', with the router switched off, to ensure that no problems arise.
• Look after the cutters and keep them sharp. Always unplug the router before changing a cutter.
• Never tighten the collet nut without a cutter fitted. This can cause serious damage to the collet, and may even break it, so always leave the nut loose.

Routing techniques

The router is, in essence, a simple machine. Its versatility stems from two main factors: the type of cutter used, and the method used to guide the machine. Much of the time, the router will be used as a hand-held tool, but there are situations where the router needs to be mounted in a purpose-made router table.

Cutters

Cutters are available in a huge range of sizes and designs to suit differing jobs and materials. Once you start doing a lot of routing, you will find that you begin to amass a large collection of cutters. Good cutters are expensive, so only buy them as you need them. It is usually a false economy to buy a set of cutters, because they often contain designs that you never use. Jigs, templates and fences to guide the router can be bought or specially made.

Cutters are commonly made from high-speed steel (HSS). The cutting edge may be tipped with tungsten carbide, in which case the cutter is known as a TCT cutter.

HSS cutters are cheaper than TCT cutters and are also capable of taking a much sharper edge. However, they are easily blunted and cannot be used on abrasive timbers and man-made boards. In general, the majority of cutters on the market are TCT, as they are extremely durable and can be used on a wide range of different materials. They can also be sharpened in the workshop using a diamond hone.

Cutter types

Straight cutters
These are parallel-sided cutters, usually with cutting edges both on the sides and the base. They are available in a variety of sizes, from a diameter of less than 2 mm (¹⁄₁₆ in) to around 50 mm (2 in). Straight cutters are used for a range of jobs, from jointing to inlaying, and are the most versatile type of cutter.

Edge-forming cutters
These are used to mould and shape the edges of a workpiece, usually for decoration. They are often self-guiding.

Jointing cutters
These specialist tools are the most complex types of cutter, and can be used for producing cabinet doors and various other joints, simply and easily. They are normally suitable for use only in a router table.

Trimming cutters
These are straight cutters with guide bearings that can be used to follow templates or trim laminates and veneers.

Guiding the router

The router must be steered precisely into the work-piece to produce accurate results. There are several methods of achieving this.

Side fence

The simplest method is to use the side fence, which will follow the edge of a workpiece. However, this will only work on straight edges, and its use is limited by the length of the mounting bars.

Trammel bar

To cut circles or arcs, a trammel bar or circle-cutting jig can be used. These are ideal for shaping circular tabletops.

Guidebush

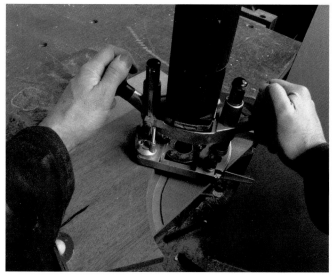

Another method is to use a piece of equipment called a guidebush, which fixes on to the base of the router. The cutter protrudes through the centre

of the guidebush and can then be used to follow a shaped template, or used with a specialist jig such as a dovetailing jig.

Bearing-guided cutters

These cutters are self-guiding and will run along the edge of a shaped workpiece without needing a fence or any additional guide. They produce consistent results.

Guide batten

For cutting housings and grooves in the centre of boards, a timber guide batten (or a pair of battens) may be used. The router base-plate can be run along the side of the batten or sandwiched between a pair of battens, so there is no chance of it wandering off-line.

Working freehand

Occasionally, the router may be used freehand for operations such as carving letters or decorative features. This is something that you can practise, as it will help develop your control of the router. Use a V-groove cutter on a piece of scrap timber and make a shallow cut. Observe how the cutter tries to pull the router off-line and how the grain pattern affects this.

Router tables

The router table is probably the most useful accessory that you can get for your router. It will allow you to use the larger jointing and moulding cutters, provided that you have a powerful enough router, and also to undertake operations that are either difficult or dangerous to attempt using a hand-held router.

A good router table must have a flat and supportive surface, the larger the better, and a sturdy fence. A sliding mitre fence is also useful, especially for moulding end-grain. The router is mounted underneath the table and it should still be reasonably easy to change the cutters. Setting the depth of cut can be a problem, because as the router is inverted, the power of the return springs and gravity both work against you. A fine height adjuster can be fitted to your router to ease these difficulties. For safety reasons, a separate power switch should be fitted to the front of the table in a convenient position, so that the router can be easily controlled. The machine's own power

switch should be permanently fixed in the 'on' position when table-mounted. Router tables are available commercially, though it is not difficult to make your own.

Dust extraction

Sawdust is a serious hazard for woodworkers. The image of the grey-haired craftsman toiling away in his workshop, up to his knees in shavings and sawdust, might evoke a romantic nostalgia, but the reality is rather different. Not only does sawdust make a terrible mess of your workshop, it can also affect your health. Inhaling the dust produced by hardwoods and man-made boards such as MDF will cause irritation and can lead to serious illness. Try to remove as much dust as possible at source, by connecting your router to a dedicated workshop vacuum cleaner. These machines are specifically designed to cope with fine dust and also often incorporate features such as automatic switching, which means that the vacuum operation can be controlled with the power switch on the router.

Other tools and equipment

Any woodworking project requires a basic set of tools in addition to your router. You will have more success if you work with timber that has been accurately cut to size and planed to a consistent thickness. To do this efficiently, you need the right tools.

High-quality workshop machine tools undoubtedly give the best results for speed and accuracy. However, good machines are expensive, take up a lot of space and are really beyond the means of most home woodworkers. Hand-held power tools are a good alternative and increased competition has reduced prices. It is now possible to buy good-quality equipment for a modest outlay. You will also need a small selection of hand tools, and measuring and marking instruments.

Measuring and marking

You will need a flexible steel tape **(1)** and a steel rule **(2)** for general measuring. A try square **(3)** and combination square **(4)** are necessary for marking out, and a compass and protractor **(5)** will also come in useful. For marking angles, a sliding bevel **(6)** is used. As you become more proficient, you may wish to invest in a mortise gauge **(7)** and a marking gauge **(8)**. Another extremely useful tool is the digital calliper **(9)**, which can be used for accurate measurements of cutters, timber thickness, rebate depths etc. Finally, you will need an endless supply of sharp pencils **(10)**.

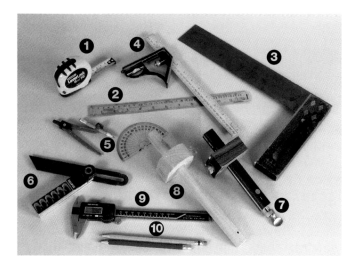

Saws

Several saws are needed, to cut both straight-edged and curved components. It is particularly important to purchase good-quality saws as these are the most frequently used tools in woodworking. For straight crosscutting (cutting across the grain of the timber), use a cross-cut saw or a tenon saw **(1)**. For ripping large boards and sheet material, a bigger saw is needed – a hardpoint saw is a good compromise **(2)**. This is not expensive and cuts well; however it cannot be resharpened. For cutting curves, use a coping saw **(3)**. This is a frame saw with a very fine and fragile blade. Luckily the blades are cheap and easy to replace. For really accurate angled cuts, a dedicated mitre saw **(4)** will save you endless hours of frustration.

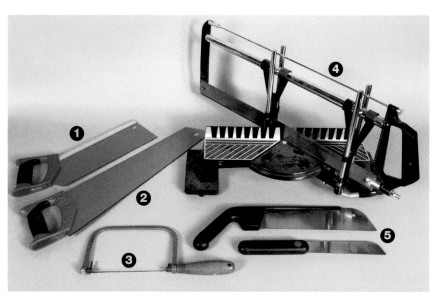

You might like to try a pullsaw **(5)**. This, as its name suggests, cuts on the pullstroke. It is easy to use and leaves a fine finish. The smaller one pictured here is very flexible and excellent for flush trimming.

Planes

A plane is needed to smooth the rough surface left by the saw, and also to prepare boards for jointing. Choose a smoothing plane **(1)** for general use and a block plane **(2)** for working on end-grain. A cabinet scraper **(3)** is also a useful tool, though it can be hard for an inexperienced user to handle.

Chisels

You will need a small set of chisels for squaring mortises and for general use. Bevel-edged chisels are the most versatile.

Screwdrivers

A selection of screwdrivers will always come in handy. Many people now opt for a powered version.

Hammers

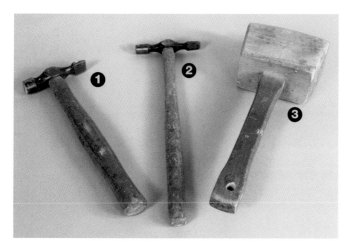

A medium-weight hammer **(1)** and a pin hammer **(2)** should cover your needs. Use a mallet **(3)** for driving chisels or persuading reluctant joints.

Clamps

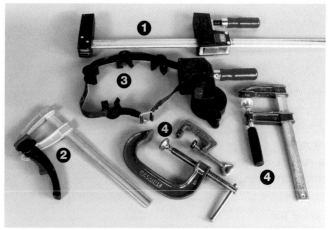

A range of clamps is also needed: bar clamps **(1)** for panels, speed clamps **(2)**, webbing clamps **(3)** for frames and F- and G-clamps **(4)** for all kinds of jobs.

Power tools

Power tools, whether mains-powered or cordless, do take a lot of the hard work out of woodwork. A power drill is a necessity and a jigsaw is also extremely useful, as it can cope with many different jobs and materials due to the wide range of available blades. A circular saw is ideal for dealing with long straight cuts. A powered planer will make short work of rough edges, and a sander will smooth and polish your projects. Sanders are available in a range of different formats. If you are only going to buy one, choose a random orbital model because it is the most versatile. One of my favourite machines is the biscuit jointer, which is basically a miniature plunge saw that is used to cut slots, into which compressed beech ovals or 'biscuits' are glued. These can be used to strengthen butt joints and replace all manner of traditional joints such as the mortise and tenon joint.

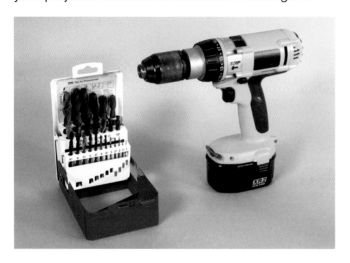

Cordless drill with set of twist drills

Jigsaw and circular saw

Planer and random orbital sander

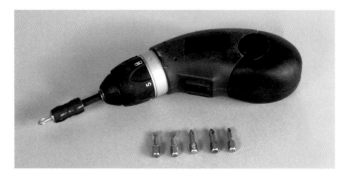

Cordless screwdriver

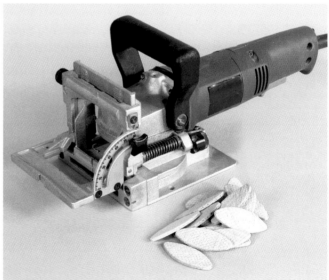

Biscuit jointer and biscuits

Basic techniques

Marking out

Measuring and marking are the two main areas where woodworking mistakes occur. There are few things more irritating than misreading a measurement and consequently cutting timber to the wrong length. There is an old saying – 'Measure twice, cut once' – and though it may sound rather trite, it really is worth keeping in mind. Once you have spoiled a couple of pieces of expensive timber, you will begin to appreciate the advice!

When marking a piece of timber, always use a try square or combination square and a sharp pencil. Mark the line around all faces of the timber to make it easier to keep your sawcut straight. When you make the cut, make sure that it is on the waste side of the line. This means that the pencil line should still be visible on the piece of timber once it has been cut.

When making several identical pieces, measure the first and then use it as a template for the others. This minimizes measuring errors, assuming that you have managed to cut the first piece to the right length. Professional makers often use devices called setting-out rods, which are effectively large boards with all the dimensions of a project marked on them. The maker then only needs to lay the timber on the board and mark off the relevant dimension.

Marking off the first face

Continuing the line onto the next face

Measuring the piece of timber

Sawing

Before you start to cut any workpiece, make sure that the wood is fixed firmly to the workbench. Alternatively, use a wooden bench hook to steady the workpiece. This is a simple piece of equipment that hooks over the edge of your workbench and stops the wood from slipping.

Crosscutting across the grain of the timber

A wooden bench hook

There are two basic sawcuts: crosscutting and ripping. Crosscutting means cutting across the grain of the timber. A tenon saw is ideal for crosscutting smaller pieces; for larger pieces, use a panel saw. Ripping is cutting along the grain, to reduce the width of a board. The panel saw or hardpoint saw may be used for this.

Start by gently drawing the blade backwards and making short, light strokes until the cut is established. Gradually increase the length of the strokes.

Ripping to reduce the width of a board

Planing

After sawing, the surface of the timber will need to be planed. A smoothing plane is a good general-purpose tool. Set it to take fine shavings, and be sure to plane with the grain – this means that the fibres in the timber are angled away from the blade, so the plane will take a slicing cut through them and leave a smooth surface. If you try to plane in the opposite direction, you will find that the plane digs in and leaves a rough surface. It can often be hard to work out the correct direction to plane in, but if you run your finger along the surface of the timber, you can usually feel which direction is the smoother (be careful not to get a splinter in your finger).

Finishing

The final processes in the making of a project are also perhaps the most important. The first thing that people notice about any piece of woodwork is its finish. As the maker, you may be very proud of your neat jointing, or your rather innovative design, but unfortunately unless the finish is perfect, these nuances will be ignored. The first thing that people do is to run their fingers over a polished surface, so it must be perfect. Wood is a very tactile material so its feel is important.

To create a good finish, preparation is vital. This means that the surface must be free from imperfections before any coating is applied. An experienced craftsman can produce a perfect surface just by using a plane; the rest of us, however, must resort to abrasives.

Sanding

Modern sanding machines can make an excellent job of smoothing the roughest surface. Abrasive papers are available in a variety of textures, from very coarse to very fine. A number followed by the word 'grit' tells you how coarse it is; the lower the number, the coarser the paper. Work through several grades of abrasive paper, starting with the coarsest and finishing with the smoothest – 240-grit paper is usually fine enough to produce a surface that is good enough to accept a finish. Final sanding should be done by hand along the grain. If timber is properly sanded it should begin to shine, as a smooth surface reflects light better than a rough one. All sharp edges should be 'softened' (sanded until they are comfortable to touch). Sharp edges are prone to splintering and chipping, and so should be avoided.

Applying the finish

Once the timber has been prepared, choose a finish. I always use an oil finish on the furniture I make as it is versatile, easy to apply, durable and can be repaired. As with any finish, the secret of achieving a good result is to build it up slowly. Start by applying a generous coat with a brush. Leave this to soak into the timber for around 15 minutes. Then take a soft cloth and wipe away any excess. Wipe along the grain and pay particular attention to corners and recesses where the oil may collect. Now leave the piece to dry for at least 12 hours.

Once the surface is dry and hard, use 320-grit abrasive paper to cut it back and remove any roughness, then apply another coat of oil, this time using a soft cloth and wiping along the grain, polishing the oil into the timber. Again leave the oil to dry, though this should not take more than about four hours. Cut back with the abrasive paper again and repeat the process. Continue doing this until the finish has built up to the desired level. As the surface becomes smoother, there is less need to use abrasive paper.

Bookends

Woodworkers can be terrible hoarders, particularly when it comes to timber, hanging on to the smallest offcuts, just in case they come in handy later. Here is a project that is an ideal way to make good use of these pieces: a pair of bookends decorated with quadrants of contrasting timber. Only a small amount of timber is needed, and the design can easily be modified to suit what you have. Two router cutters are used and there is one joint to make.

Essential tools
Measuring and marking tools
Plane
Tenon saw
Compass
Jigsaw or coping saw
Bar clamps

Router accessories
Router table
Straight cutter 18 mm (¹¹⁄₁₆ in) in diameter (smaller will do)
Bearing-guided rounding-over cutter

Cutting list
Base – 2 pieces tulipwood, 170 x 120 x 18 mm (6¹¹⁄₁₆ x 4¾ x ¹¹⁄₁₆ in)
Upright – 2 pieces tulipwood, 194 x 120 x 18 mm (7⅝ x 4¾ x ¹¹⁄₁₆ in)
Quadrants – offcuts of rosewood, American black walnut and mahogany to make 6 quadrants: 2 with a radius of 70 mm (2¾ in), 2 with a radius of 100 mm (4 in) and 2 with a radius of 130 mm (5⅛ in)

Additional materials
Abrasive paper
Glue

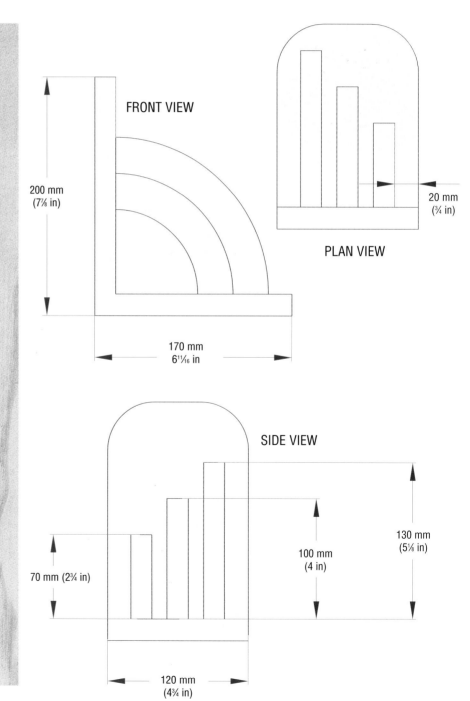

FRONT VIEW

200 mm (7⅞ in)

170 mm 6¹¹⁄₁₆ in

PLAN VIEW

20 mm (¾ in)

SIDE VIEW

70 mm (2¾ in)

100 mm (4 in)

130 mm (5⅛ in)

120 mm (4¾ in)

1 Begin by preparing the timber for the bases and the uprights. Make sure it is an even thickness and that the sides are planed square and parallel. Mark out the dimensions and cut the boards to length with a tenon saw.

2 The upright sits in a rebate that is cut into the base-board. The simplest way to mark this is by standing the upright in position on the baseboard, with its edge flush with the end. Use a sharp pencil to mark the width of the rebate on the base. Mark the depth of the rebate – it should be about 12 mm (½ in) deep.

3 The best way to cut a rebate on a small board is to use the router table. Take a straight cutter and set it as shown in the picture. The fence is set so that the cutter just reaches the marked line for the width of the rebate, and the height is set so that the cutter just reaches the marked line for the depth of the rebate. Make several shallow passes until you reach the full depth. To stop breakout, it is wise to run a backing board behind the workpiece.

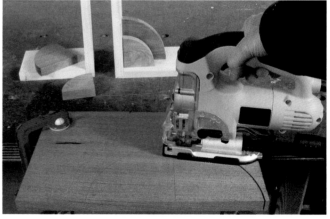

4 Choose contrasting timbers to make the quadrants. Mark out the timber with a compass. The easiest way to make a quadrant is to cut out a half-circle and then divide it in half.

5 A jigsaw is ideal for cutting out curved components such as these quadrants. However, a coping saw will do just as well. You could use the router and a jig or template to cut out the quadrants, but as there are so few to cut out, it would take more time than it is worth.

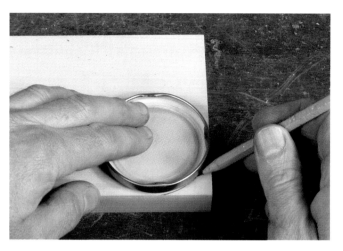

6 Once the quadrants have been cut out, smooth the edges with abrasive paper. Fit a bearing-guided rounding-over cutter in the router table, and machine the curved edges of the quadrants on both sides. Bring the fence up so that it is in line with the bearing. Use it to lead the workpiece onto the cutter. (Grip the workpiece firmly so that there is no kickback on initial contact.) The rounding-over cutter does not make a deep cut, so the machining may be done in one pass, and the workpiece will be easy to control.

7 To soften the appearance of the bookends and echo the curves of the quadrants, round over the corners of the bases and the uprights. You can buy special templates of varying sizes to help you do this, but usually the easiest and cheapest way is to find some circular object, such as a tin or jar lid, which provides the right sort of curve. Hold it over the corner of the workpiece, with its edges flush with the edges of the work, and draw around it with a pencil.

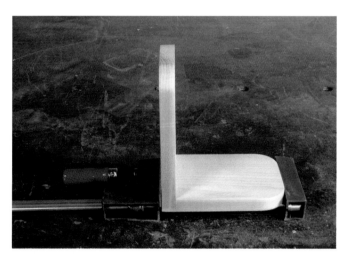

8 Cut off the corners with the jigsaw or coping saw, and then smooth the curve with a sanding block (a piece of scrap timber with a piece of abrasive paper wrapped around it). Now the main parts may be glued together. Apply a thin layer of glue to both surfaces of the rebate. Position the upright in the rebate and clamp the assembly together with a bar clamp. Make sure that the angle between the two components is 90°, otherwise it will be difficult to fit the quadrants. If you do not have a suitable clamp, a large rubber band could be used instead. Leave to dry.

9 Remove the frames from their clamps once the glue has cured. Carefully sand the faces and edges and make sure that no traces of glue are visible. Soften all the edges with fine abrasive paper. Position the quadrants and make sure that they will fit neatly. Place a piece of medium-grade abrasive paper on the bench and smooth the flat edges of the quadrants to ensure a neat joint. Before gluing in the quadrants, make sure that the grain all runs in the same direction. Apply a thin layer of glue and carefully stick the quadrants in position.

Kitchen shelves

In the kitchen, it is always a great idea to have the items you use most within easy reach. This simple set of shelves works wonderfully as a mug shelf but could easily be used for spice jars. Each shelf has a high front edge to keep everything securely in place and underneath there is a handy rail for tea towels. The shelves are traditionally jointed with housing joints, so the router cutter and timber must be the same thickness. The timbers used are ash and rosewood.

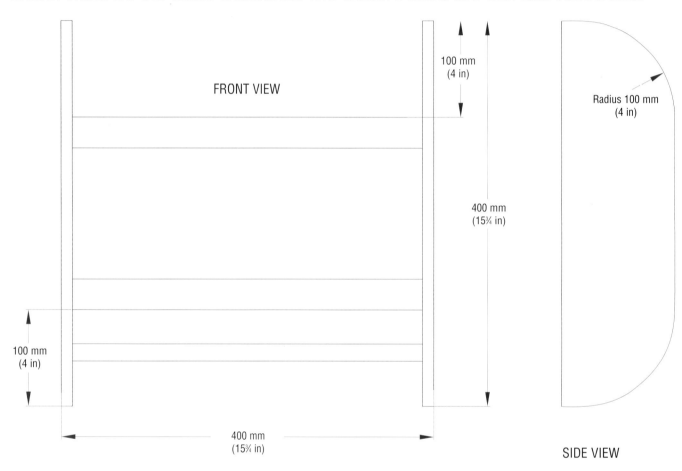

FRONT VIEW

100 mm (4 in)

400 mm (15¾ in)

Radius 100 mm (4 in)

100 mm (4 in)

400 mm (15¾ in)

SIDE VIEW

Essential tools
Measuring and marking tools
Ripsaw
Steel rule
Chisels
Saw
Bar clamps
G-clamps
Tenon saw or pullsaw

Router accessories
Straight cutters: 12.7 mm (½ in), 6 mm (¼ in) and 18 mm (¹¹⁄₁₆ in)
Bearing-guided rounding-over cutter

Cutting list
Sides – 2 pieces ash, 400 x 120 x 12.7 mm (15¾ x 4¾ x ½ in)
Shelves – 2 pieces ash, 400 x 110 x 12.7 mm (15¾ x 4⁵⁄₁₆ x ½ in)

Dowel – 1 piece 18 mm (¹¹⁄₁₆ in) in diameter, 400 mm (15¾ in) long
Shelf fronts – 2 pieces rosewood, 388 x 30 x 10 mm (15¼ x 1³⁄₁₆ x ⅜ in)

Additional materials
Glue
Abrasive paper
Metal mounting brackets

1 Start by cutting the main components to length. Make sure that the ends are square and the sides are parallel. Line up the two side boards and mark out the position of the housings where the shelves will join.

2 Because the sides are wider than the shelves, the housings do not run their full width. Lay a shelf on top of the side, with the two back edges lined up. Mark the width of the shelf on the side. This marks the end of the housing.

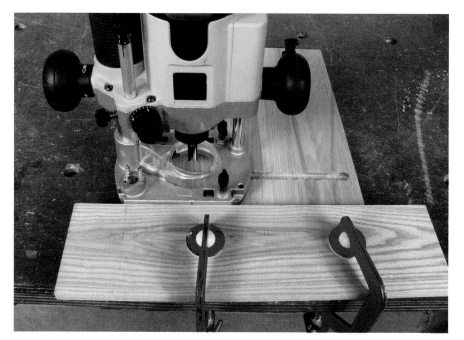

3 The housings are routed out using a straight cutter of exactly the same thickness as the shelves, in this case 12.7 mm (½ in). Set the depth of cut to 6 mm (¼ in). You can cut the joints in both sides at the same time. Line up the boards, back to back, and make sure that the ends are perfectly level. Clamp a guide batten across the two boards with the G-clamps to guide the cutter exactly along the marked line. To make the cut, work from the right-hand side to the left – the cutter spins clockwise so it will keep pushing the router against the guide batten. If you move the router in the other direction, the cutter will be trying to pull the machine away from the batten all the time, and you will risk making an inaccurate cut.

4 After routing, the ends of the housings will be rounded. Square them off with a chisel.

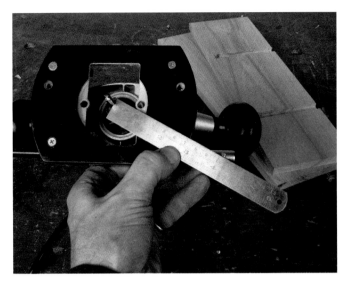

5 To cut the curves on the ends of the side panels, use a trammel attachment on the router. This is simply a point that attaches to one of the fence rods, and around which the machine may be pivoted. Fit the router with a fairly small straight cutter of around 6 mm (¼ in) in diameter. Use a steel rule to set the radius to 100 mm (4 in).

6 Place the side panel on the workbench on top of a piece of scrap timber or sheet material. Mark a line 20 mm (¾ in) in from the back edge and around 100 mm (4 in) from the end. Clamp the panel to the workbench with the G-clamp.

7 Place the router on the workpiece and position the trammel point on the marked line. Lower the cutter to touch the surface and adjust the position of the machine so that the inside edge of the cutter just overhangs the end of the board. Swing the router around the trammel point and ensure that the cutter will exit smoothly from the front edge of the board. Once you are happy with the settings, you can make the cut.

8 Make several shallow passes until you finally cut into the scrap board below. Be sure to keep the pressure on the inside edge of the router to keep the trammel point firmly in the timber.

9 A piece of hardwood dowel is used for the rail. The router can be used to bore the hole for this. Fit a straight 18 mm (¹¹⁄₁₆ in) cutter and mark the position of the rail on the side panels with a cross. It should be set 50 mm (2 in) in from the back and 50 mm (2 in) up from the bottom edge. Set the depth of cut to 6 mm (¼ in). The router will cut a very neat hole, but it can be difficult to hold it still while making the cut so use the side fence coupled with a G-clamp. Set the side fence to position the centre of the cutter exactly 50 mm (2 in) in. Clamp the board to the workbench, and put the router in position over the mark. Use a small G-clamp to hold the router securely in place. Depending on the design of the router and side fence, it may be tricky to get the clamp in place. You may find it easier to let the board overhang the side of the workbench a little.

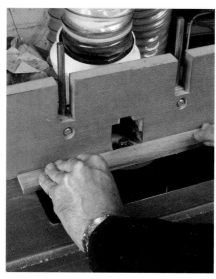

10 The next job is to round over the sides and the shelf fronts. Fit the router table with the bearing-guided rounding-over cutter and set the fence level with the bearing. Raise the cutter so that it will create a good radius.

11 Cut the shelf fronts roughly to length and round over the top edges on both the inside and outside faces.

12 Round over both the side boards on the inside and outside faces. Be careful when routing the curved sections, because the end-grain will scorch if you move too slowly.

13 Before fitting the shelf fronts, it is worth cutting a shallow rebate on the backs of them. Use the 12.7 mm (½ in) straight cutter (or a larger one) in the router table, and use an offcut from the end of one of the shelves to set the width of the rebate. Hold the offcut above the cutter and push the fence back until the front of the cutter is just flush with the front face of the offcut. Lock the fence in position and set the cutter about 4 mm (3/16 in) above the table. Carefully cut the rebate on the inside of both the shelf fronts.

14 Assemble the shelves and measure the exact length of the shelf fronts, then cut the fronts to length with a tenon saw or pullsaw.

15 Apply glue to the housings and the holes for the rail. Assemble the shelves and clamp up with a pair of bar clamps in line with the shelves. Measure across the diagonals of the assembly to ensure that it is square. Both diagonals should be of equal length. If they do not match, loosen the clamps and realign the shelves before tightening the clamps again.

16 Once the main assembly is dry, the shelf fronts can be glued in place. Use a pair of clamps on each shelf to hold it in place until the glue dries. Finally, sand all surfaces and apply a finish. To attach the shelves to a wall, use a pair of metal mounting brackets, available from most hardware stores.

Table lamp

Good lighting is an essential part of any home and table lamps are a great way to light up the corners of a room. Here is an elegant design that makes the most of the router's decorative abilities. It takes the form of a square column with fluted faces. Both the base and the top are moulded using a bearing-guided cutter. A light fitting is screwed to the top. Alternatively, a larger hole may be bored in the top and the same design used to make a candlestick.

Essential tools
Measuring and marking tools
G-clamps and spring clamps
Tenon or pullsaw
Power drill
Jigsaw
Screwdriver

Router accessories
Router table
Cove cutter: 10 mm (⅜ in) in diameter
Bearing-guided chamfer cutter
Bearing-guided ogee cutter or similar

Cutting list
Top – 1 piece oak, 70 x 70 x 20 mm (2¾ x 2¾ x ¾ in)
Base – 1 piece oak, 150 x 150 x 20 mm (5¹⁵⁄₁₆ x 5¹⁵⁄₁₆ x ¾ in)
Column sides – 1 piece oak, 950 x 46 x 12 mm (37⁷⁄₁₆ x 1¹³⁄₁₆ x ½ in)
Eventual dimensions of each side are 210 x 46 x 12 mm (8¼ x 1¹³⁄₁₆ x ½ in)
Blocks – 2 pieces mounting 25 x 25 x 25 mm (1 x 1 x 1 in)
Holding jig – 1 piece scrap board, 250 x 200 mm (9⅞ x 7⅞ in)

Additional materials
Abrasive paper
Glue
Lamp fitting and cable to suit
Adhesive pads (optional)
Lampshade

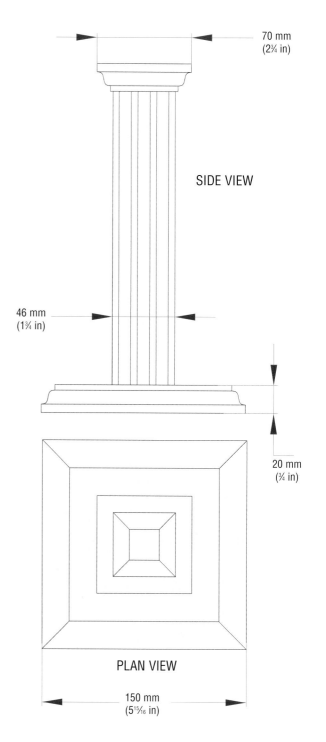

70 mm (2¾ in)

SIDE VIEW

46 mm (1¾ in)

20 mm (¾ in)

PLAN VIEW

150 mm (5¹⁵⁄₁₆ in)

HELPFUL HINT

The column is made from four lengths of timber, with three flutes routed into them. The most difficult part of this project is getting the flutes evenly spaced. Experiment on a timber offcut until the spacing looks right. Remember that you only need to set the side fence twice, because both the outside flutes may be cut using the same setting, by reversing the workpiece.

1 Using a ruler, square and pencil, mark out the flute positions for the sides of the lamp on the single length of timber for the column (there will be enough waste at the end to allow you to clamp it securely to the workbench).

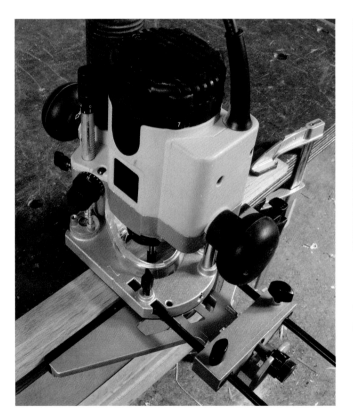

3 Fit the cove cutter and make a series of short cuts, adjusting the settings until you are happy with the result. The flutes should be about 4 mm (³⁄₁₆ in) deep and may be cut in one pass.

2 Clamp the workpiece to the edge of the work-bench, making sure that it overhangs slightly, so that the side fence will not touch the bench itself.

4 Having finalized the settings, you can now mould the sides. Do not cut the sides to length before moulding them.

5 The sides will be joined using a mitre joint – use a bearing-guided chamfer cutter for this. The angle of this cutter is 45°, so it will produce a perfect mitre joint. When moulding the edge of a narrow workpiece, it is preferable to use a router table for safety and accuracy. Set the cutter height so that there is about 1 mm (1/32 in) of the workpiece running against the bearing.

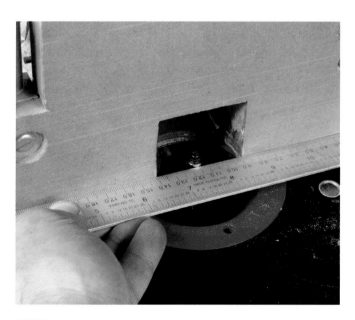

6 Use a straight-edge to set the router table fence exactly level with the bearing.

7 Mould both edges, making sure that the flutes are facing upwards. Be careful to keep your hands well away from the cutter.

8 Now cut the sides to length. Use a try square and a pencil to square the end.

9 Carefully make the cut using a fine-toothed saw.

10 Mitre joints can be difficult to glue, however the fluting on these makes it fairly easy. Run a thin line of glue down one face of the joint and press the two halves together. Make sure that the joint lines up on both ends. Secure it using small sprung clamps or even clothes pegs (which should locate easily in the flutes). Alternatively, adhesive tape can be used.

11 All four sides can be glued at the same time. Make sure that the column is perfectly square and set it aside until the glue has cured. Cut the two pieces for the top and the base to size and make sure they are square and that the edges are smooth. Fit the bearing-guided ogee cutter to the router table and mould the edges of the base. Start on the end-grain and work in a clockwise direction so that you finish on the side grain. This will ensure that you end up with no breakout on the corners.

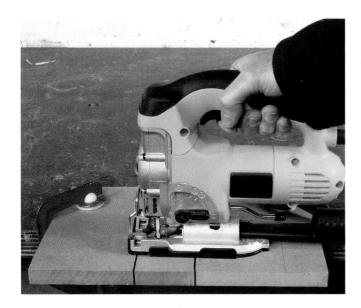

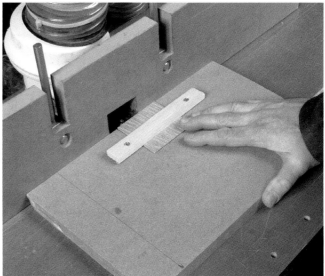

12 Moulding the top is a little more complicated. Because it is so small, it is not safe to mould it freehand. You need to make a simple holding jig from a piece of scrap board. Take the top and place it on the board so that its side is flush with the long side of the board. Draw around it with a pencil. Cut out the waste with the jigsaw.

13 The top should slot snugly into the cut-out in the board, and the edge must line up. Screw a thin timber batten across the top to hold it down. Now start the router and run the whole board past the cutter. Take out the top, turn it round and replace it. Repeat the process until all four sides have been moulded.

14 To assemble the lamp, you first need to make up two small blocks with sides approximately 25 mm (1 in) long. These should be adjusted so that they fit snugly into the ends of the column. Once you are happy with the fit, glue one block in the centre of the base and the other onto the underside of the top. When the glue has cured, drill a hole (large enough to take the electric cable) through the centre of both blocks.

15 You need to provide clearance for the cable under the base. This can be done either by using the cove cutter to make a straight cut from the centre hole to the edge of the base, which is deep enough to contain the cable or, alternatively, you could stick adhesive pads on the underside of the base to raise it up and provide space that way. Before finally gluing the components together, install the cable and fit the light fitting. Refer to a qualified electrician if necessary.

Tray

This tray has endless uses – from breakfast in bed to drinks in the garden. It is simple to make and exploits the router's jointing capabilities. The frame and the base have been made from contrasting timbers – American black walnut for the frame and chestnut for the base – but any timbers may be used. Mitre joints are used at the corners: these must be accurately cut, so you will need a sharp saw with a good mitre guide. The final finishing is also important, because the tray will be handled a lot and so it must feel smooth and comfortable to hold.

Essential tools
Measuring and marking tools
Try square
Powered jigsaw or coping saw
Vice
Rip saw
Crosscut saw with mitre guide
G-clamps
Band clamp or adhesive tape
Block plane

Router accessories
Router table
Straight cutters: 6 mm (¼ in) and 9 or 10 mm (⅜ in)
Bearing-guided (or pin-guided) rounding-over cutter
Slotting cutter: 4 mm (³⁄₁₆ in)
V-groove cutter

Cutting list
Side – 2 pieces American black walnut, 600 x 40 x 9 mm

(23⅝ x 1⁹⁄₁₆ x ⅜ in)
End – 2 pieces American black walnut, 380 x 70 x 9 mm (15 x 2¾ x ⅜ in)
Base – 5 pieces chestnut, 600 x 85 x 9 mm (23⅝ x 3⁵⁄₁₆ x ⅜ in)
Jig – 1 piece MDF, 250 x 60 x 12 mm (9⅞ x 2½ x ½ in)

Additional materials
Abrasive paper
Glue

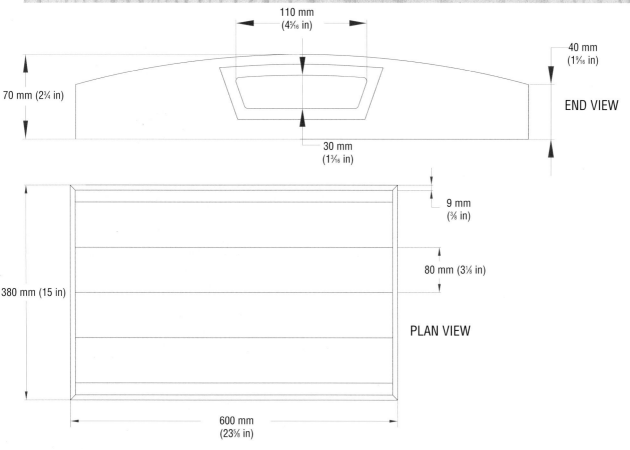

110 mm
(4⁵⁄₁₆ in)

40 mm
(1⁹⁄₁₆ in)

70 mm (2¾ in)

END VIEW

30 mm
(1³⁄₁₆ in)

9 mm
(⅜ in)

80 mm (3⅛ in)

380 mm (15 in)

PLAN VIEW

600 mm
(23⅝ in)

1 Start by preparing the two ends of the frame. These are the most demanding parts to make, because you have to make the curves and the handles match. Mark out the timber with the length of the component and then mark the height at the ends, 40 mm (1⁹⁄₁₆ in), and the height at the centre, 70 mm (2¾ in). To produce a smooth curve through these three points, take a thin piece of timber or plywood and gently flex it with your hands at either end, so that it bends evenly. Hold it over the workpiece so that it passes through the three points, and then get a helper to draw the curve on the timber.

2 Cut out the curve using either a powered jigsaw or a coping saw, as shown here. Do not square the ends yet, but leave the piece over-long. Use it as a template to mark out the other end and cut it out as well. However well you manage to follow the marked line, there will still be some discrepancies between the two ends. Clamp them together in a vice and, using a sanding block, smooth the edges until they match. Prepare the two side pieces, but leave them a little over-long and also slightly wider by about 2 mm (¹⁄₁₆ in). This will be planed off later.

3 The base of the tray is held in a groove that is routed into the inside faces of the sides and the ends. Choose a cutter to match the thickness of the baseboards, ideally about 10 mm (⅜ in). Fit it into the router table and set the cutter height to 4 mm (³⁄₁₆ in) above the table. The distance from the fence should also be about 4 mm (³⁄₁₆ in). Make a test cut on a waste piece to verify the settings. Then cut the groove on the inside face of all four components.

4 Now cut all four sides to length. The joint is a mitre joint, and the easiest way to cut this is to use a dedicated mitre saw. However, you can also use a tenon saw with a mitre box. Again, if you are unsure about the accuracy of your saw, make a test cut using scrap pieces, so that you can then make adjustments if necessary.

MAKING A HANDLE JIG

The next job is to cut out the handle holes in each end. You could easily do this freehand with a coping saw or jigsaw; however, it really does look neater if both are identical. To ensure this, spend five minutes making a jig. For this job you need a straight cutter, 6 mm (¼ in) in diameter is ideal, and a guidebush fitted to the router base.

To make the jig, first draw round one of the ends on the piece of MDF. Then draw the position of the handle. Calculate the difference between the cutter and the guidebush in order to determine the template size. For example, if the guidebush is 24 mm (¹⁵⁄₁₆ in) (in diameter and the cutter is 6 mm (¼ in) in diameter, halve the two sizes and subtract the smaller from the larger – the difference here is 9 mm (⅜ in). So draw a line around the handle exactly 9 mm (⅜ in) outside the existing line, and cut this out with a jigsaw. To help locate the end piece in the jig, pin three thin timber strips on the MDF. The end piece will now fit precisely into the jig. Fix it in place with a couple of clamps at the ends.

Invert the jig with the end piece clamped in position, and fix the whole assembly to the edge of the bench so that it overhangs. Fit the router with the 6-mm (¼-in) cutter and the guidebush.

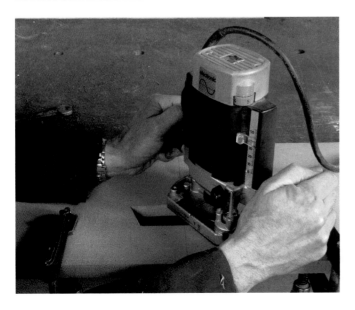

5 Make a handle jig (see above). Before making the cut, place the router on the jig, with the power off, and move it around the recess to make sure that its path is clear and that the clamps do not get in the way. Ensure that the power cable is also safely positioned. To cut out the handle, place the router in the recess with the guidebush hard against the edge. Start the motor and plunge the cutter so that it just goes into the workpiece. Move the router smoothly around the jig in a clockwise direction until you have completed one circuit. Release the plunge lock and plunge the cutter a little further into the work, then repeat the circuit. Continue until you break through. Keep the router moving evenly so that you do not burn the timber, and make several shallow passes.

6 The handles must be comfortable to hold so the timber must be smooth and rounded. Use a bearing- or pin-guided rounding-over cutter fitted in the router table to machine both sides of the handle. Because of the shape of the handle, the cutter will not be able to reach right into the corners, so you will have to finish these with a piece of abrasive paper. The frame is now complete.

7 The boards for the base could simply be laid edge to edge in the frame, but a more attractive solution is to use tongue-and-groove joints. You can buy dedicated cutter sets to cut these joints, but they tend to be expensive and only suitable for a limited range of timber thicknesses. I prefer to use a slotting cutter, which can be used to cut both parts of the joint, and then form the decorative chamfer using a V-groove cutter.

8 To cut the grooves you will need to work on the router table. Always cut the groove first, as it is much easier to make a tongue to fit a groove, rather than vice versa. Set the cutter in the table so that it lines up with the centre of the board thickness. Adjust the fence so that the groove depth is 5 mm ($\frac{3}{16}$ in). Check the settings, then cut a groove on one edge of each of the baseboards.

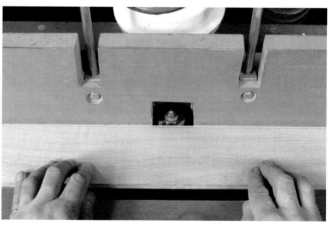

9 To cut the tongue, reset the cutter using the groove as a guide. Do not touch the fence setting, but simply lower the cutter in the table until its top edge lines up with bottom edge of the groove. This setting is a little fiddly to get right, so do experiment on offcuts first.

10 Cut the tongue in two passes by making one cut on one edge and then flipping over the board and making a second cut on the other edge. This ensures that the tongue is centrally positioned on the board.

11 To finish the baseboards, you need to put a small chamfer on either side of the joint. The reason for this is to make a feature of the joint rather than try to conceal it. It also has the effect of making it more difficult to see if there is any discrepancy between the gaps of the individual joints. Use the V-groove cutter and set it as shown in the picture. Make sure that it does not cut into the tongue. Reset the fence and do the same to the grooved edge.

12 Trim and arrange the boards ready for assembly. Crosscut them to length first and then set them out with four full-width boards across the centre and two narrow boards on either side. The two side boards will need to be ripped to width. Make sure that you do this evenly, so that the boards are centralized across the tray. When all the boards are joined together, they should be a slightly loose fit across the tray to allow for any expansion.

13 To strengthen the tray frame, you can glue both the outside boards into the side grooves.

A section through the board after the routing has been completed

14 Now assemble all the parts. Apply a little glue to each of the corner joints and the ends of the outer boards. Make sure that no glue gets into the end grooves or onto any of the other baseboards.

15 Clamp the tray using a band clamp. Once the glue has cured, remove the clamp and clean up the edges. The sides need to be planed down to match the angle of the end pieces. Do this with a block plane, working from both ends. Finally, go over the whole piece with abrasive paper.

Shoe rack

How do you store your shoes? If your family is anything like mine, shoes are scattered all round the house, carefully positioned to trip you over. Here is a design for a proper shoe rack to keep them all tidied away. It is extremely simple to make, but also solid and reliable. Beech has been used for the sides and cherry for the rails, but you can use any timber that you like, and a mix of timbers can be attractive. The jointing is straightforward and a pocket hole jig is used to bore the ends of the support rails for easy attachment to the side panels.

Essential tools
Measuring and marking tools
Tenon saw
Bench hook
F- or G-clamp
Pocket hole jig
Plane
Sander
Drill and drill bit: 4 mm ($\frac{3}{16}$ in)
Screwdriver

Router accessories
Router table
Bearing-guided chamfer cutter
Straight cutter: 20 mm ($\frac{3}{4}$ in)

Cutting list
Side – 2 pieces beech,
400 x 300 x 20 mm
($15\frac{3}{4}$ x $11\frac{13}{16}$ x $\frac{3}{4}$ in)
Rear rail – 2 pieces cherry,
710 x 30 x 20 mm ($27\frac{15}{16}$ x $1\frac{3}{16}$ x $\frac{3}{4}$ in)
Support rail – 4 pieces cherry,
670 x 50 x 20 mm
($26\frac{3}{8}$ x 2 x $\frac{3}{4}$ in)

Additional materials
Abrasive paper

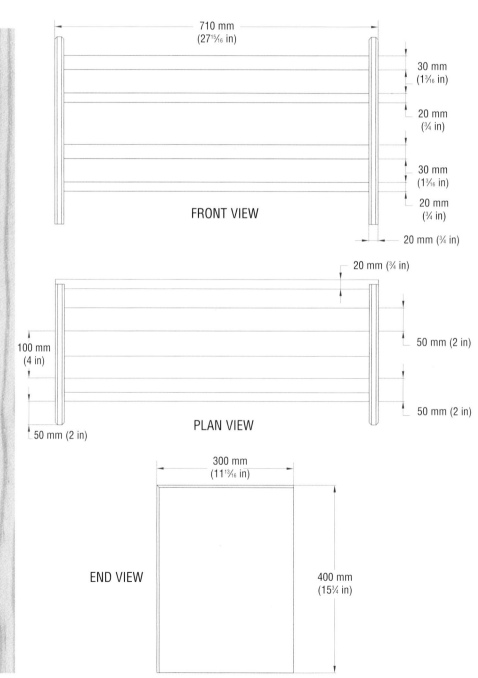

710 mm
($27\frac{15}{16}$ in)

30 mm
($1\frac{3}{16}$ in)

20 mm
($\frac{3}{4}$ in)

30 mm
($1\frac{3}{16}$ in)

20 mm
($\frac{3}{4}$ in)

FRONT VIEW

20 mm ($\frac{3}{4}$ in)

20 mm ($\frac{3}{4}$ in)

100 mm
(4 in)

50 mm (2 in)

50 mm (2 in)

50 mm (2 in)

PLAN VIEW

300 mm
($11\frac{13}{16}$ in)

END VIEW

400 mm
($15\frac{3}{4}$ in)

1 Start by cutting the side panels to size and make sure that the edges are square and true. Mark out and cut the rear rails exactly to length. Use a tenon saw and a bench hook for an accurate result.

2 Place the rails on the workbench, and stand the side panel vertically across them, making sure that the ends are flush with the outside face of the side panel. Use a pencil to mark the width of the panel on the rail. You only need to do this on one rail end.

3 Take the combination square and mark a line along the centre of the thickness of the rail. This is obviously 10 mm (⅜ in) from the edge. This measurement is not critical and a millimetre or so either way will make little difference.

4 Fit the straight cutter to the router table. Put the marked rail on the table and raise the cutter up to the level of the marked centre-line. Set the fence back so that the outer edge of the cutter just reaches the shoulder (vertical) line.

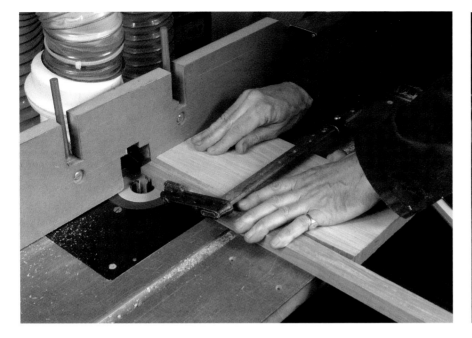

5 It is not safe to try to mould the end of a narrow rail without support. You can either use a sliding mitre fence or, alternatively, a timber support block. The support block can be any piece of reasonably wide scrap timber. It must, however, have an accurately cut square end. Use a clamp to fix the rail to the front of it and make sure that the rail end and the block square end are absolutely level. Make the cut by running the block along, hard against the fence, and push the rail through the cutter. Let the cutter cut into the support board.

6 This is what the joint looks like after machining. The support board ensures that you get a clean cut without any break-out from the back of the rail.

7 Once you have machined the four ends of the rear rails, place one on the workbench and use it to mark the precise length of the supporting rails. These should be identical in length to the shoulder lines on the rear rails. Align the end of the supporting rail with the shoulder on the rear rail, and mark the other end with a square and a pencil.

8 Mark out the positions of all the supporting rails on the inside faces of the side panels. Use one of the rails to simplify the process.

9 For ease of assembly, the rails are screwed into the side panels from the inside. To do this accurately, you need to use a pocket hole jig. These are very simple to use and once set according to the manufacturer's instructions, it is just a matter of clamping each rail in the jig and drilling a pair of holes through the end. Make sure that you drill all the holes on the underside of the rails.

10 To add a little decoration to an otherwise rather stark structure, use the bearing-guided chamfer cutter to mould the edges of all the components. Fit the cutter to the router table and line up the fence with the roller bearing.

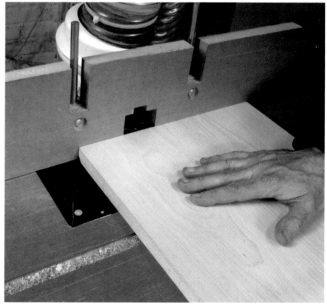

11 Mould both the upper edges of the support rails and the front upper and lower edges of the rear rails.

12 Mould the top and the front edges of the side panels. Mould the top edge first and finish on the front. Mould both the inside and outside faces.

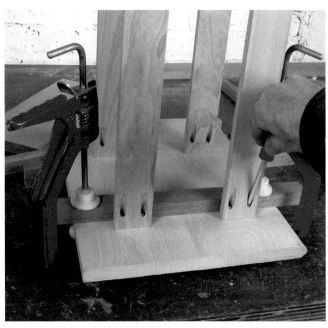

13 Sand all the rails smooth and start to assemble the rack. Place a side panel on the workbench with its inside face upwards. Clamp a batten across it along the line where the rails are to fit. This is to ensure that the rail doesn't move while the screws (which are set an an angle) are tightened. Place a rail in its marked position and screw it to the panel tightly.

14 Continue this process until all the rails are fixed in place on both side panels.

15 Stand the rack on the workbench and fit both of the rear rails in place. Drill through the rail into the side panel and fix with one screw on each end.

Knife block

Kitchen knives need to be easily accessible, and it is important to store them safely. A knife block is a great solution. You can design one to hold all your knives and keep them sharp and ready for use. Here is a simple design that you can customize to suit your needs. It has been made in American black walnut and American white ash, but you can use any hardwood offcuts that are lying around the workshop.

Essential tools
Measuring and marking tools
Crosscut saw and ripsaw
Bar clamps
Mallet
Sander
Chisel
Plane
G-clamp
Band clamp

Router accessories
Side fence
Straight cutter: 19 mm (¾ in)
Bearing-guided rounding-over
cutter

Cutting list
24 lengths (in total) of American
black walnut and American
white ash, 300 x 20 x 20 mm
(11¹³⁄₁₆ x ¾ x ¾ in)

Additional materials
Glue
Abrasive paper
Oil to finish
Adhesive rubber feet

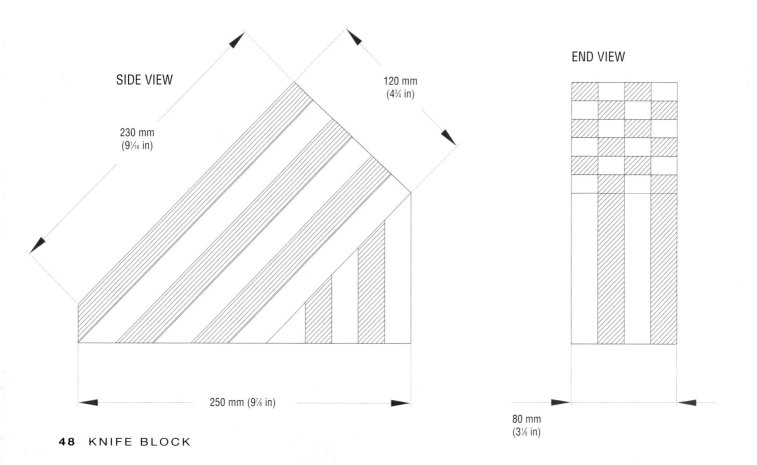

SIDE VIEW

120 mm
(4¾ in)

230 mm
(9¹⁄₁₆ in)

250 mm (9⅞ in)

END VIEW

80 mm
(3⅛ in)

1 Prepare all the timber. All the pieces should be the same length and thickness. They will be glued together to make four panels of six pieces.

2 Spread glue evenly on each piece and clamp the assembly tightly in a pair of bar clamps.

3 If you have a large pair of clamps, you can clamp up all four panels at the same time. Try to make sure that each piece is level and in line with the next. As you tighten the clamps, the pieces are inclined to slip a little, so re-check and tap into place with a mallet if necessary. Once the glue has set, remove the panels from the clamps and clean up with a sander until the surface is smooth. If there are any large lumps of dried glue, clean them off first with a chisel.

4 Once the boards are smooth, decide how to arrange your knives in the block. Stand the boards on their ends and sandwich the knives between them. Mark their position on the ends of the boards.

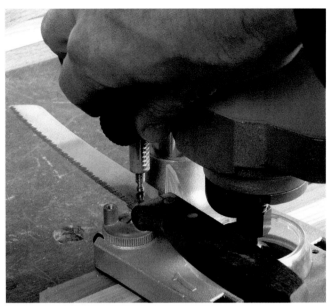

5 Lay the boards flat on the bench and mark out the width of each blade on the inside. Make sure that you leave enough space for curved blades, otherwise the knife handle will not sit squarely in the block when the knife is inserted.

6 Use the knife blade itself to set the depth of cut on the router. Insert the cutter and plunge the router down, with the power off, so that the cutter is just touching the workpiece. Sandwich the knife blade in the depth adjuster as shown in the picture, then open it another millimetre or so to make it easy to insert and remove the knife.

7 One difficulty with routing boards of this length is that there is little space for the clamps. If you are careful, you can simply use one clamp. Start by clamping the board on the far end. Make sure that the edge of the board overhangs the bench edge.

8 Start routing the groove until the router contacts the clamp. Stop and reposition the clamp on the front end of the board and finish the cut. If the groove needs to be wider than the cutter width, reset the side fence and repeat the process.

9 When all the grooves have been routed, glue all the boards together. Spread the glue evenly on each board.

10 Clamp up all the boards tightly. Use as many bar clamps as you can to ensure a really good bond.

11 Once the glue has cured, remove the bar clamps and clean up the sides with the sander. Lay the longest knife on the block to determine the length it needs to be. Use a combination square to mark a 45° cut on the base of the block. Extend the line around the edges of the block.

12 Cut off the end of the block as cleanly as possible using a tenon saw.

13 Do not discard the waste piece as it will be used to give added support to the block. Plane and sand the cut end so that it will join neatly onto the main piece. Trim it to fit.

14 Liberally coat the support piece with glue. End-grain is very absorbent and this will not be an enormously strong joint (it does not actually need to be).

15 Because the block is an irregular shape, this is a slightly difficult joint to clamp up. The easiest method to use is a band clamp. Alternatively, a webbing roofrack strap with a ratchet buckle can be used.

16 Smooth the base of the knife block with a sander. Make sure that it is completely level, so that the block will stand on a flat surface without rocking or wobbling.

17 Finally, you need to treat all the sharp edges. Fit the bearing-guided rounding-over cutter to the router and mould all the edges. Clamp the block to the workbench and work around the block, moving the clamp as necessary. To protect the base of the block from any kitchen worktop spills, attach a set of four adhesive rubber feet to support it.

Jewellery box

Making boxes is a great way to use up small amounts of timber and there are lots of interesting ways of decorating and personalizing a box. This small jewellery box is made from American ash, which is a very pale timber. The corners are decorated with spline dovetails made from bog oak, which is ancient timber that has been immersed in a bog for hundreds of years and has consequently turned jet black. However, any two contrasting timbers will work equally well. To insert the splines, you will need to make a simple jig on which to run your router.

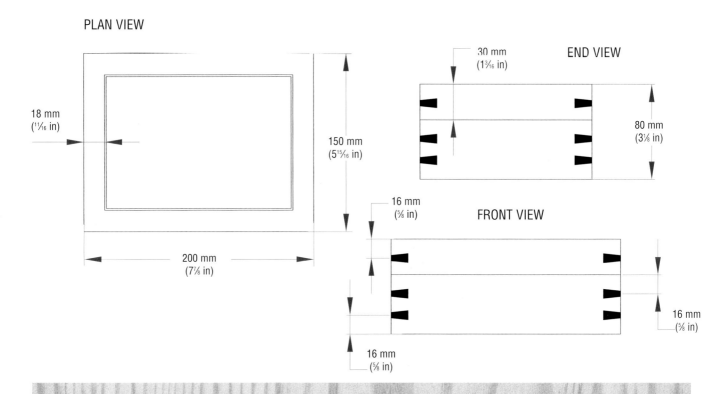

PLAN VIEW

18 mm
($1\frac{1}{16}$ in)

150 mm
($5\frac{15}{16}$ in)

200 mm
($7\frac{7}{8}$ in)

30 mm
($1\frac{3}{16}$ in)

END VIEW

80 mm
($3\frac{1}{8}$ in)

16 mm
($\frac{5}{8}$ in)

FRONT VIEW

16 mm
($\frac{5}{8}$ in)

16 mm
($\frac{5}{8}$ in)

Essential tools
Measuring and marking tools
Mitre saw and tenon saw
Flexible pullsaw and hacksaw
Band clamp
Bench vice
Hammer
Power sander
F- or G-clamps
Screwdriver

Router accessories
Router table
Small dovetail cutter: 8 mm
($\frac{5}{16}$ in) in diameter

Straight cutter: 6 mm ($\frac{1}{4}$ in)

Cutting list
Side – 2 pieces American ash, 200 x 80 x 18 mm ($7\frac{7}{8}$ x $3\frac{1}{8}$ x $\frac{11}{16}$ in)
Side – 2 pieces American ash, 150 x 80 x 18 mm ($5\frac{15}{16}$ x $3\frac{1}{8}$ x $\frac{11}{16}$ in)
Top – 1 piece American ash, 170 x 125 x 12 mm ($6\frac{11}{16}$ x $4\frac{15}{16}$ x $\frac{1}{2}$ in), approx.
Base – 1 piece plywood or MDF, 180 x 130 x 6 mm ($7\frac{1}{16}$ x $5\frac{1}{8}$ x $\frac{1}{4}$ in), approx.
Spline dovetails – 1 piece bog

oak, 350 x 40 x 12 mm (14 x $1\frac{9}{16}$ x $\frac{1}{2}$ in)

Jig top plate – 1 piece MDF, 360 x 200 x 18 mm ($14\frac{3}{16}$ x $7\frac{7}{8}$ x $\frac{11}{16}$ in)

Jig frame – 2 pieces MDF, 180 x 100 x 18 mm ($7\frac{1}{16}$ x 4 x $\frac{11}{16}$ in) and 100 x 100 x 18 mm (4 x 4 x $\frac{11}{16}$ in)

Additional materials
Glue
Panel pins: 12 mm ($\frac{1}{2}$ in)
Abrasive paper
Piano hinge

1 Prepare the timber. Ideally, have one length of timber that can be cut up to make all four sides. This makes it easy to machine. Select a well-figured piece for use on the top. Take the length of timber for the sides and mark the thickness of the top on it. Mark the rebate for the base panel. This should be 6 mm (¼ in) wide and 10 mm (⅜ in) high.

2 Using the router table, cut a groove 6 mm (¼ in) wide by 5 mm (³⁄₁₆ in) deep just inside the line that you marked for the top. Also machine the rebate for the base panel.

3 When the routing is complete, cut the sides to length using a mitre saw. Roughly assemble the sides and measure the size of the top into the grooves. The top panel should be cut to be a little undersized across the grain, to allow for any expansion.

4 Fit the straight cutter in the router table and machine a rebate around the edge of the top panel. The height of the cutter should be set to produce a tongue 6 mm (¼ in) thick to fit the groove, and the width should be set to produce an even space around the top panel when it is assembled in the frame. This may involve a certain amount of trial and error, so set a narrow width to start with and increase it as necessary.

5 Lay out the components of the box (base and four sides), ready for assembly.

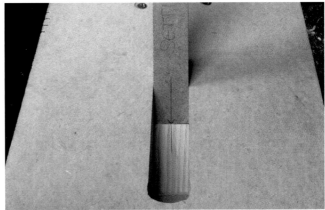

6 Fit the top panel into the grooves in the sides and, being careful not to get any glue on it, glue all the mitre joints. Clamp the assembly using a band clamp, and make sure that the top panel is centrally positioned. Make a jig for the insertion of the spline dovetails (see box).

7 Mark out the position of the splines as shown in the drawing. Use the setting bar on the jig to align the centre of the slot with the marked line. Clamp the box in position and secure the whole assembly in the bench vice.

Making the jig

To support the router and guide it through the corners accurately, a jig is needed. It must be made to suit your router. This version was made to fit a router with a 24-mm (¹⁵⁄₁₆-in) guidebush.

The jig components are made from 18-mm (¹¹⁄₁₆-in) MDF, though ply would do equally well. Begin by cutting the top plate to size. Mark the centre of the board, and rout out a recess that exactly matches your guidebush. Use the side fence to guide the router and a straight cutter to make narrow passes until the recess is just wide enough to contain the guidebush without any play. Don't worry if the recess is slightly off-centre.

The frame below the top plate consists of four components. Make sure that the angle between the supports is exactly 90° and that the top plate sits on it at precisely 45°. The boards do not need to be as wide as the top plate: 100 mm (4 in) should be adequate.

Once the boards have been cut to length and mitred, cut a slot in the mitred ends – make it the same width as the guidebush and about 40 mm (1⁹⁄₁₆ in) long. This is where the cutter will pass through the side of the box, so you need good clearance.

Glue and screw the jig tightly together. Pre-drill the MDF to avoid splitting the core, and counter-sink the screws so that they won't foul the router.

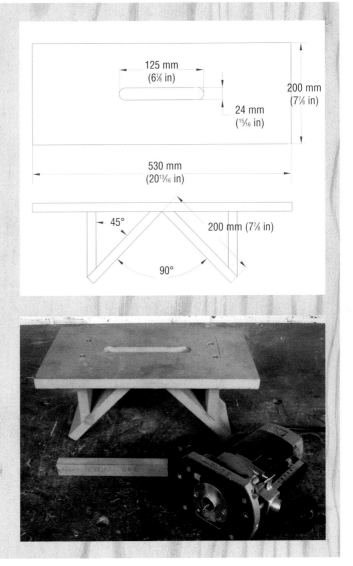

125 mm (6⅞ in)

24 mm (¹⁵⁄₁₆ in)

200 mm (7⅞ in)

530 mm (20¹³⁄₁₆ in)

45°

200 mm (7⅞ in)

90°

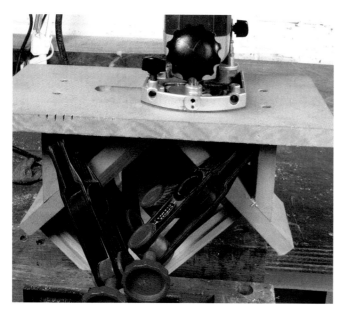

8 Fit the router with the dovetail cutter and the guidebush. Place it on the jig, and with the power off, centre it over the box and plunge the cutter so that it just touches the top of the corner. Lock it down and then set the depth stop to make a pass about 10 mm (⅜ in) deeper than this. Release the router and pull it back to the front of the slot. Plunge the machine to the depth you have set and engage the plunge lock. Start the motor and run it gently along the slot, cutting through the corner of the box. Move slowly to ensure that you make a clean cut without causing any breakout as the cutter exits the timber. Turn off the router without releasing the plunge lock, and once the motor has stopped, lift it out of the jig, reset the jig on the next line and repeat the procedure until all the corners have been machined.

9 Once you have routed all four corners, the box is ready for the splines. To make the splines, fit the router in the router table and use the dovetail cutter again. You are aiming to make one long length, which can then be cut up to fit in the routed slots.

10 Set the dovetail cutter as shown, just protruding past the fence, so it makes a shallow cut. Make a pass on each side of the board and then check the fit in the routed slots. Reset the fence a fraction further back and make another pass if the timber is too large. Continue this process until the spline is a tight fit in the slot. Ideally, it should be tapped in with a hammer. When you are happy with the fit, saw off the moulded edge of the board and cut into short lengths.

11 Check the fit of the splines. Cut the splines roughly to length and glue in position. Once the glue has dried, trim off the end of the splines with the pull-saw. If you do not have one, a tenon saw may be used, but be careful not to damage the side of the box. Finally, sand down the splines with a power sander, or use a sanding block.

12 Carefully cut the base of the box to size, so that it is a snug fit in the rebate. Apply a little glue to the rebate and pin the base in place with panel pins.

13 It is now time to cut off the top of the box. Mark a line around the box, in pencil, exactly 30 mm (1³⁄₁₆ in) down from the top. Set the box on its side on the workbench and secure it with the F- or G-clamp. Take the tenon saw and carefully work around the line, turning the box as you go.

14 Once the lid has been parted, take a piece of abrasive paper and clamp it to the workbench. Smooth the edges of both the box and the lid to remove any unevenness, until both parts fit neatly together.

15 The final job is to fit the hinge. There are many different types of hinge that you could use, but probably the easiest to fit is the piano hinge. These hinges are available in a variety of lengths, but you will probably need to trim it to length using a hacksaw. The hinge should be positioned with the knuckle protruding out of the back of the box. Mark the position of the hinge on the back of the box and cut a shallow rebate on this line using the router table.

16 The rebate should be deep enough to accommodate the thickness of the hinge leaf plus the fixing screw. Screw the hinge in place.

Wastepaper bin

A smart wastepaper bin makes all the difference to a room, whether it is an office or a living room. Here is a modern design that should be at home in almost any situation. With its elegantly sloping sides and contrasting timbers, it is almost too good to put rubbish in. The timbers are sweet chestnut and American black walnut.

Essential tools
Measuring and marking tools
Hardpoint panel saw
Plane
Tenon saw or pullsaw
Bar clamp
Webbing clamp
G-clamp
Screwdriver

Router accessories
Router table
Straight cutter: 10 mm (⅜ in)
Bearing-guided chamfer cutter

Cutting list
Corner posts – 4 pieces
American black walnut,
400 x 30 x 20 mm (15¾ x 1³⁄₁₆ x
¾ in)

Panels – 4 pieces sweet chestnut, 250 x 300 x 10 mm (9⅞ x
11¹³⁄₁₆ x ⅜ in)

Additional materials
Abrasive paper
Glue
Screws: 3 x 13 mm (⅛ x ½ in)

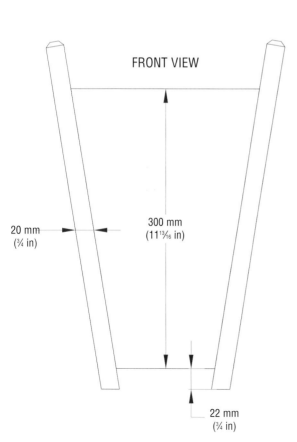

FRONT VIEW

50 mm
(2 in)

20 mm
(¾ in)

300 mm
(11¹³⁄₁₆ in)

22 mm
(¾ in)

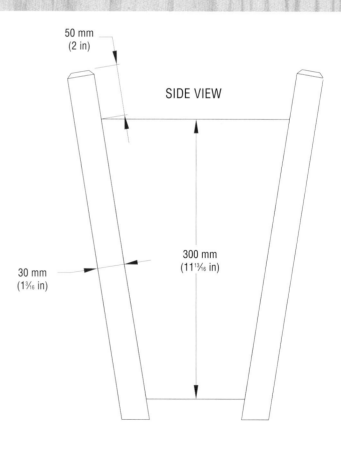

SIDE VIEW

30 mm
(1³⁄₁₆ in)

300 mm
(11¹³⁄₁₆ in)

1 Start by marking out the side panels. To save material, the panels are arranged side by side with every alternate one inverted. The grain of the timber should run across the panels. Leave a small space between them to allow space for the sawcut.

2 Carefully cut out the panels with the hardpoint saw. Clean up the edges with a plane if necessary. Mark out the position of the panels on the corner posts. The corner posts should be cut to 400 mm (15¾ in) in length. Mark the central point and then measure and mark a point 145 mm (5¾ in) each side of this. The total length of the groove for the panel is 290 mm (11⁷⁄₁₆ in). Carry these end marks around the posts.

3 Fit the straight cutter into the router table. Set the depth of cut to 6 mm (¼ in). Using one of the corner posts, line up the cutter so that it is in the centre of the face that is 20 mm (¾ in) wide. This setting is not critical, but try to get it as near as possible.

4 As the groove is not going to run the full length of the post, you need to fit stop blocks to the router fence to prevent the marks being overrun. Place the post on top of the cutter, with the power off. Position it so that the front mark is just over the front tip of the cutter. Clamp a block onto the fence so that it is just in contact with the back end of the post. Tighten the clamp and check the setting. Now repeat the process with the back mark, and this time clamp a block onto the fence at the front end of the post.

5 To cut the grooves, care is needed. Start the router and place the post with its back end hard against the rear block, while holding the front end well above the cutter. Keeping it tight against the fence, lower the post onto the cutter and let it plunge in until the post is flat on the table. Then push the post forwards until it contacts the front block. Carefully lift it off the cutter, keeping it tight against the fence. Repeat the process on the adjacent face and on the other three posts.

6 The groove is deliberately cut a little too short to accommodate the panel. This is to allow a small overlap on the panel at either end, to cover the end of the groove should any shrinkage occur. Therefore you need to cut a small notch on either end of the panels. To work out the size of the notch, push one panel into the groove and, using a sharp pencil, mark the depth on the panel. Take the panel out and put it beside the post. Mark the length of the groove on the panel, and then make a mark 5 mm (³⁄₁₆ in) or so back on either end.

7 Cut out the notches using a tenon saw or pull-saw. Assemble the bin without gluing, to check for any problems.

8 The next job is to level the feet. While the bin is still assembled, stand it on a level surface and mark around each foot using a rule. Make sure that the side of the rule is flat against the bench.

9 Dismantle the bin and carefully trim the ends of the feet to the marked lines. Sand the ends smooth.

10 The tops of the posts are chamfered on all four sides. End-grain moulding is tricky to do so use a supporting board to stop the workpiece slipping into the cutter. Fit the bearing-guided chamfer cutter into the router table and adjust the depth of cut. Align the fence with the guide bearing using a metal rule. Take a square-ended timber offcut and clamp it to the back of the post. Make sure that the ends of both pieces are exactly in line, and that the clamp is a safe distance from the cutter.

11 To make the cut, start the router and holding the board and the post hard against the fence, run it past the cutter. Let the cutter mould the end of the post and cut into the supporting board. Remove the post from the board, turn it over, re-clamp and repeat the process until all four edges are moulded. Repeat on all the posts.

12 The posts are now finished and the final job before assembly is to fit supporting blocks to hold the base panel. These are simply short lengths of timber, 10 mm (⅜ in) square, glued to the bottom inside edge of the panels.

13 Glue the posts onto two panels and leave them to dry, and then glue the other two panels in place. Do not use too much glue here, because the posts are fitted across the grain of the panels and must not restrict any movement. Only glue the centre portion of the panel into the groove. Do not glue more than one-third of the panel length.

14 Clamping up a tapered assembly is awkward, because the clamps will simply slide off. Here is a simple solution. Firstly, clamp both assemblies together with a bar clamp to give two parallel sides for the clamp to work on. You will encounter another problem as you tighten the clamp – the two centre posts will slide out of line. To stop this happening, take a piece of folded abrasive paper and sandwich it between the posts before applying the clamping pressure. This will stop them moving.

15 You do not need to use great pressure to hold these panels together. Use a single bar clamp and tighten it just enough to push the panels fully into the grooves.

16 Once the glue has cured, the second pair of panels can be glued in place. Holding the assembly together is difficult – the solution is to use a webbing clamp or a roofrack strap. Wrap it around the centre of the two previously glued panels to hold the other panels in position. Do not over-tighten.

17 Finally, make the base panel. This is made from an offcut of sweet chestnut but you could easily use plywood. The tapered sides make it difficult to measure, and the corners have to be notched to suit the posts so it is a good idea to make a cardboard template first.

18 Fix the base panel in position with a pair of screws through the supporting battens.

Mirror

Routers are particularly good at creating lengths of moulding, and with a small selection of cutters you can build up some impressive examples. This makes it easy to make your own frames for paintings, photographs or mirrors. The moulding on the frame of this swivelling dressing table mirror is made using a single cutter for both sides, and a pair of rebates is cut on the inside to accommodate the mirror and the back panel. The design of the base has been kept plain, using the same cutter again for the edge moulding.

Essential tools
Measuring and marking tools
Jigsaw or coping saw and mitre saw
Band clamp
Drill
Drill bits: 2-, 3-, 4- and 5-mm (¹⁄₁₆-, ⅛- and ³⁄₁₆-in)
Screwdriver
G-clamp

Router accessories
Router table
Bearing-guided rounding-over cutter
Straight cutter: 12 mm (½ in)
Bearing-guided chamfer cutter

Cutting list
Base – 1 piece English cherry, 410 x 190 x 20 mm (16⅛ x 7½ x ¾ in)
Support posts – 2 pieces English cherry, 300 x 30 x 25 mm (11¹³⁄₁₆ x 1³⁄₁₆ x 1 in)
Mounting blocks – 2 pieces English cherry, 70 x 20 x 10 mm (2¾ x ¾ x ⅜ in)
Frame sides – 2 pieces American black walnut, 400 x 30 x 20 mm (15¾ x 1³⁄₁₆ x ¾ in)
Frame ends – 2 pieces American black walnut, 260 x 30 x 20 mm (10¼ x 1³⁄₁₆ x ¾ in)
Back panel – 1 piece plywood or MDF, 380 x 240 x 6 mm (15 x 9⁷⁄₁₆ x ¼ in)

Additional materials
Glue
Abrasive paper
Mirror: 4 mm (³⁄₁₆ in) thick, cut to siz
Screws: 10 x 12 mm (½ in) and 200 x 70 mm (2¾ in) long
Washers

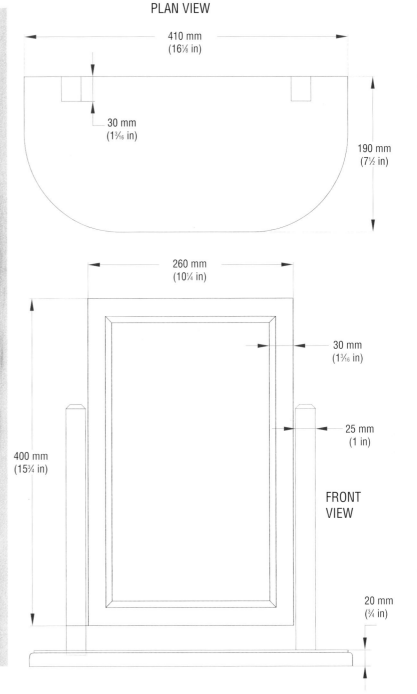

PLAN VIEW

410 mm
(16⅛ in)

30 mm
(1³⁄₁₆ in)

190 mm
(7½ in)

260 mm
(10¼ in)

30 mm
(1³⁄₁₆ in)

400 mm
(15¾ in)

25 mm
(1 in)

FRONT VIEW

20 mm
(¾ in)

1 Cut the base to size with the crosscut and rip-saws. The ends need to be rounded. You can use templates or a compass, but the easiest way to do this is to find something circular that seems about the right diameter, such as a saucepan lid, place it over the corner and draw around it. Cut around the corners with a jigsaw or a coping saw.

2 The top edge of the base is moulded using a bearing-guided rounding-over cutter. Set the cutter sufficiently high in order for the vertical edge on the lower part of the cutter to cut into the surface. This gives a more defined edge. It is called a quirk.

3 To make the frame, prepare the timber to the size in the cutting list, but do not cut to length at this stage. You need to cut two rebates on the inside face. First cut the one for the mirror itself using the straight cutter. This should be 10 mm (⅜ in) deep and about 5 mm (³⁄₁₆ in) wide. This assumes that your mirror is 4 mm (³⁄₁₆ in) thick and the back panel is 6 mm (¼ in) thick.

4 Cut a second rebate. Move the fence back another 5 mm (³⁄₁₆ in) or so and reduce the cutter height to cut a rebate 6 mm (¼ in) deep. Be careful doing this, as you are reducing the support underneath the work-piece. This makes it more liable to tip into the cutter, so guide the timber carefully past the cutter.

5 Having completed the rebates, replace the straight cutter with the bearing-guided rounding-over cutter and using the same setting that you used on the base, mould the inside edge of the front of the frame.

6 Lower the cutter and mould the opposite side of the frame so it just rounds over the edge without forming a quirk.

7 Once the moulding is complete, cut the frame components to length using the mitre saw.

8 Glue and clamp the frame using a band clamp. Meanwhile, make the supporting posts for the mirror. Prepare to the dimensions in the cutting list but, as always, leave over-long. The sides of the posts are left square-edged but the tops are chamfered.

Moulding end grain

Moulding end-grain can be fraught with difficulties, particularly on narrow components. Do not try to do it freehand, as it will end in disaster. The tip of the workpiece will catch on the cutter and you will not get a smooth cut. The simplest way to complete this cut is to clamp the post to a wider board. It is extremely important that this board has a perfectly square end. Hold both pieces hard against the fence and clamp up as shown in the picture. Alternatively, you can use a mitre fence with a supporting board behind the workpiece.

9 The bearing-guided chamfer cutter is used for this operation. Set the fence in line with the bearing, and the cutter high enough to take a reasonable chamfer. Start the router, run the workpiece slowly past it and let the cutter run into the backing board.

10 Stop the router, remove the post, turn it over and repeat the process until all four edges have been moulded. The tops of the posts should look like this.

11 Take the assembled frame to your local glazier so the mirror can be cut to fit.

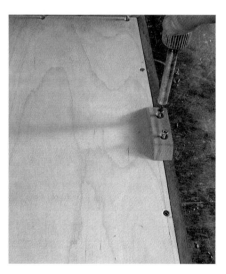

12 Cut the back panel to size so that it fits in the rebate. The back panel is screwed into place, so it is easy to replace the mirror. Drill holes, 3 mm (⅛ in) in diameter, around the panel and countersink them. Put three across the bottom and top, and two on each side. The centre of the sides will be covered by the mirror mounting blocks, so no fixing screw is needed. Screw the panel in place with the 12-mm (½-in) screws.

13 The mirror is suspended between the two posts on a pair of mounting blocks. You can mitre the ends on the mitre saw to improve their appearance, though as they will rarely be seen, this is not vital. Drill and countersink a pair of 3-mm (⅛-in) holes through the faces of them, and also bore and countersink a 4-mm (³⁄₁₆-in) hole through the side.

14 Screw the blocks in position on the rear of the mirror frame, so that they are exactly on the centre-line and flush with the outer edges of the frame.

15 Measure and mark the position of the mirror pivot points on the supporting posts. They should be 230 mm (9⅟₁₆ in) from the base, and in the centre of the post. Drill a 2-mm (⅟₁₆-in) pilot hole in both posts. Lay the mirror face down and screw through the mounting blocks into the posts. Place a thin washer on the screw between the mounting block and the post to provide a little clearance and stop the mirror frame hitting the posts.

16 Measure the position of the posts on the assembled frame and transfer this measurement to the base. Mark a central point on each position and drill a 5-mm (³⁄₁₆-in) hole through the base. Countersink on the underside.

17 Mark the centre-point on the base of each post and drill a 3-mm (⅛-in) pilot hole. Be careful to keep the drill exactly in line with the post, otherwise it will be difficult to position the post accurately.

18 Finally, lay the mirror on its back and screw through the base into the posts. Use 70-mm (2¾-in) screws and put a dab of glue on the end of each post for added security.

Side table

A simple side table can find a home in almost any room. This elegant design, with tapering legs and edge-moulded top, is quick and easy to make, using simple jointing. To shape the legs, you will need to make a jig for use on the router table. As a finishing touch, you might like to try inlaying the top with a decorative line.

Essential tools
Measuring and marking tools
Crosscut and ripsaws
Biscuit jointer
Plane and sander
Chisel
Drill and drill bits: 4 mm (³⁄₁₆ in) and countersink
Screwdriver
Clamps
Pair of toggle clamps

Router accessories
Router table
Straight cutters: 6 mm (¼ in) and 1.5 mm (¹⁄₁₆ in)
Bearing-guided chamfer cutter
Bearing-guided profile cutter
Inlay cutter

Cutting list
Legs – 4 pieces English cherry, 635 x 30 x 30 mm (25 x 1³⁄₁₆ x 1³⁄₁₆ in)
Rails – 2 pieces English cherry, 390 x 90 x 19 mm (15⅜ x 3⁹⁄₁₆ x ¾ in)
Rails – 2 pieces English cherry, 260 x 90 x 19 mm (10¼ x 3⁹⁄₁₆ x ¾ in)
Top – 1 piece English cherry, 510 x 380 x 19 mm (20¹⁄₁₆ x 15 x ¾ in)
Buttons – 10 pieces cherry, 40 x 20 x 19 mm (1⁹⁄₁₆ x ¾ x ¾ in)
Leg-tapering jig – 1 piece MDF, 800 x 160 x 12 or 18 mm (31⁷⁄₁₆ x 6¼ x ½ or ¹¹⁄₁₆ in)

Additional materials
Glue
Screws: 4 x 25 mm (1 in)
Inlay line: stained boxwood, 2500 mm x 1.5 mm (100 in x ¹⁄₁₆ in)
Abrasive paper

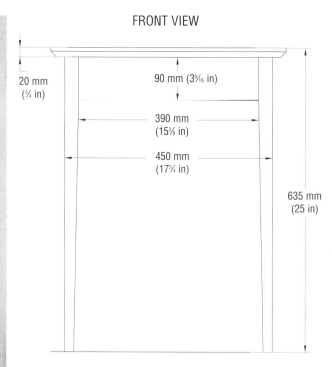

FRONT VIEW

20 mm (¾ in)

90 mm (3⁹⁄₁₆ in)

390 mm (15⅜ in)

450 mm (17¾ in)

635 mm (25 in)

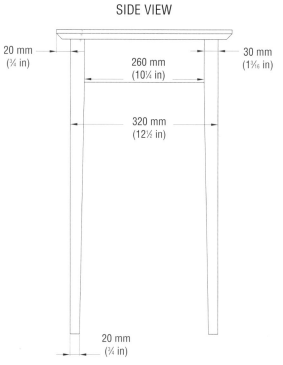

SIDE VIEW

20 mm (¾ in)

260 mm (10¼ in)

30 mm (1³⁄₁₆ in)

320 mm (12½ in)

20 mm (¾ in)

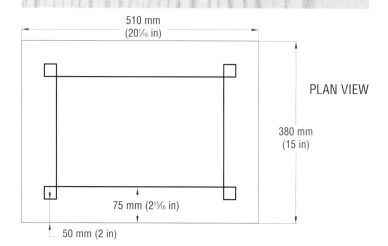

510 mm (20¹⁄₁₆ in)

PLAN VIEW

380 mm (15 in)

75 mm (2¹⁵⁄₁₆ in)

50 mm (2 in)

1 Prepare the timber for the frame and cut to length. The legs are left square at this stage. Biscuit joints will be used to assemble the frame because they are quick and easy to make. First, mark the position of the joints on the rails. They should be centrally placed, so set the combination square to 45 mm (1¾ in).

2 Mark the legs. Keep the same setting on the combination square and measure down from the top. Remember to mark two adjacent faces.

3 Set the biscuit jointer so that the biscuit position is roughly located in the centre of the board thickness, and cut all the joints on the rail ends. Clamp the rails securely to the workbench when machining them, and make sure that you hold the jointer level.

4 Before cutting the joints on the legs, raise the jointer fence by 5 mm (³⁄₁₆ in). This will set the joint back to the middle of the leg and give a much better appearance.

5 Clamp the legs to the workbench and cut the joints.

6 The cutter used with the jig is a template profiler, which is a straight cutter with a bearing matching the diameter of the cutter mounted on the shank. The bearing is guided by the shape of the jig or template, so that the cutter will reproduce the shape.

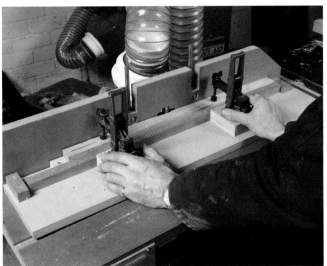

7 Set the cutter height so that the bearing is running securely on the baseboard of the jig.

8 The fence should be set in line with the cutter bearing, so that the body of the cutter is protected by it. Start the router and use the toggle clamps as hand-holds. Run the jig past the cutter and make a shallow pass. Take care, as the cutter can plunge too deeply if you are not careful. Continue machining the edge until it is smooth. Roll the leg over in the jig and repeat the process. Remember to taper only the inside faces with the biscuit slots.

TAPERED LEG JIG

The tapering jig is a useful workshop aid. It may be easily modified to cope with a variety of leg sizes and taper angles, simply by resetting the guide battens. To taper the legs accurately, a special jig is needed. This can be made from a few pieces of MDF; the only hardware that you need is a pair of toggle clamps to hold the leg in position.

Start with the baseboard. One long edge must be perfectly straight and true in order for the cutter bearing to run against it. Refer to the picture and note how the jig is set out. You need one long batten, roughly 25 mm (1 in) square and 615 mm (24⅜ in) or more long. You also need two short lengths of batten to use as end stops.

Mark the position of the long batten adjacent to the true straight edge; mark a point 20 mm (¾ in) in from the edge close to one end of the baseboard. Now measure along the edge 515 mm (20¼ in), and mark a point exactly 30 mm (1³⁄₁₆ in) in. Draw a line between these two points and that

is where the batten should be fixed. Place a short batten at the foot end and then put a leg blank into the jig. This must be cut exactly to length. Take the second short batten, butt it up tightly against the top of the leg, and screw into position.

Now simply fix the toggle clamps in suitable positions to hold the leg securely for routing. Make sure that they are set back so that they cannot come into contact with the cutter.

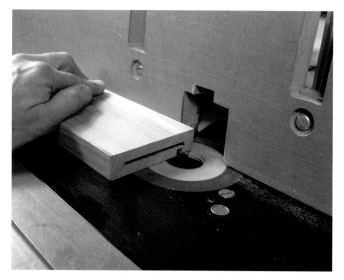

9 Once all the legs have been machined, the final job before assembling the frame is to cut a groove in the top of the rails. This is needed to locate the timber 'buttons' that will be used to hold the top in position. Again use the router table and insert the 6-mm (¼-in) straight cutter. This should be set with its outside edge about 19 mm (¾ in) from the fence; its depth should be 5 mm (³⁄₁₆ in). The grooves may all be cut in one pass. Make sure that you are machining the top inside face of each rail.

10 The frame components, ready for assembly.

11 Tackle the assembly in two stages. Start by gluing the two long rails and the legs. Apply the glue to the biscuit slots and then insert the biscuits. Put a little glue on the end of the rail and assemble the joints. Use just enough glue for a tiny amount to be squeezed out as the joint is assembled, but do not overdo it as this can cause problems when it comes to applying a finish to the table. Wipe away any surpus glue with a damp cloth.

12 Carefully clamp up both assemblies, making sure that the rails are flush with the tops of the legs, and set them aside to dry.

13 Once the glue has dried, finish the frame by fitting the cross-rails. Stand the frame on a level surface when doing this and ensure that it is all square as you tighten the clamps. Compare the diagonal measurements from corner to corner – they must be exactly equal.

14 The top is made up from several boards biscuit-jointed together. It is then cut to size and the edge is moulded with the bearing-guided chamfer cutter.

15 Do the moulding in a series of passes. Always start on the end-grain and work around the board finishing on the side grain; this prevents breakout. Keep making passes until you have a well-defined chamfer around the underside of the board.

16 Make the buttons that will be used to fix the top in place. They are made from short lengths of board that are rebated on the end. Take a board and mark out the rebate. The width should be 5 mm (³⁄₁₆ in) and the protruding tongue on the end should be 6 mm (¼ in) thick, to match the groove in the rails. Have a trial run and check the fit. If it is no good, you can always simply saw the tongue off the end and then reset the router and try again until you are happy with the fit.

17 After machining, cut the timber to length – about 40 mm (1⁹⁄₁₆ in). Cut the buttons to width – about 20 mm (¾ in). The precise dimensions of the buttons are not critical, as long as they are large enough to locate in the groove and screw securely into the underside of the tabletop. Drill a clearance hole in each button, 4 mm (³⁄₁₆ in) in diameter, and countersink for neatness.

18 Mark out the position of the frame on the underside of the top. Mark the position of the corners with a pencil.

19 Line up the frame with the pencil marks and screw the buttons into position. Put three along the short rails and two along the long ones. The buttons on the short rails may be pushed right into the bottom of the groove, but on the longer rails leave a little space, so that there is room for the top to expand to cope with changes in humidity.

INLAYS

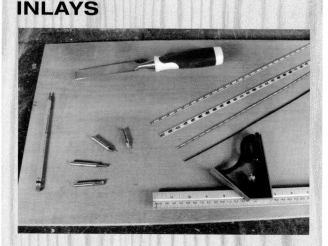

Inlaying used to be a fairly demanding operation but with a router, it becomes much easier. Inlaying involves cutting a groove in a surface and inserting a contrasting timber or decorative line into it. This is then smoothed to match the surrounding surface. Inlay lines are available in a wide range of designs and sizes, and router cutters are made to match standard sizes.

This side table has an inlaid stained boxwood line, which really is not difficult to do. Begin by preparing the surface of the table: it must be properly sanded and smooth. Carefully mark out the position of the line. You do not need to mark all round. The most important points are the corners – it is vital not to rout your groove too long, otherwise the table will be ruined. Use a combination square with the length set at 50 mm (2 in) to mark the corners.

20 Fit the router with the 1.5-mm (¹⁄₁₆-in) straight cutter and place it on the tabletop. Adjust the side fence so that the cutter is exactly 75 mm (2¹⁵⁄₁₆ in) from the table edge. To set the depth of cut accurately, carefully plunge the cutter, with the power switched off, until it just touches the surface. Lock the router down and take a short length of the inlay. Place it on top of the depth-setting turret and wind the depth adjuster down until the inlay is tightly sandwiched between the two. Lock the depth adjuster in place and remove the inlay. Now the router depth is set correctly.

21 Pull the router back to the corner mark and make sure that the cutter is just inside it. Keep the fence firmly against the edge, start the motor and plunge the cutter. Slowly cut the groove along the table. Make sure that you stop before you get close to the end line. Repeat this on the other three sides and then reset the router fence to 50 mm (2 in) from the side.

22 Cut the last two short sides of each corner. Again, be careful not to overshoot the marked line. The corner should now look something like this. The ends of the grooves will be left rounded by the router cutter. You need to square all these off with a chisel before the inlay can be fitted.

23 To make a neat corner joint, the ends of the inlay must be mitred. The simplest way to do this is to use a combination square and a chisel. Trap the inlay line under the square and make sure that it is hard against the reference fence. Place the flat side of the chisel against the rule and snip off the end of the inlay. As long as the chisel is sharp, this will produce the perfect mitre.

24 Apply a tiny amount of glue to the base of the groove using a sliver of wood or a pin. Press the inlay into place with the flat side of a chisel. Sometimes the groove and the inlay are not a perfect match, and the inlay will not fit. You need to sand the inlay's sides between your fingers to reduce the width.

25 Work slowly around the groove. Be patient and do not worry if you have cut a piece the wrong length, because you can always lever it out and replace it. The inlay should stand slightly proud of the surrounding surface.

26 The inlay must be smoothed carefully. Do not use abrasive paper, as this will rub black dust from the line into the light wood surrounding it and turn the surface a muddy grey. Use a sharp chisel or a cabinet scraper and shave off the top until the surface is level and smooth.

Cupboard

Making cabinets is easy with a router: fitting shelves, making panelled doors and recessing of hinges are all easily accomplished. This small, wall-hung cabinet incorporates a traditional inset panelled door and an internal shelf.

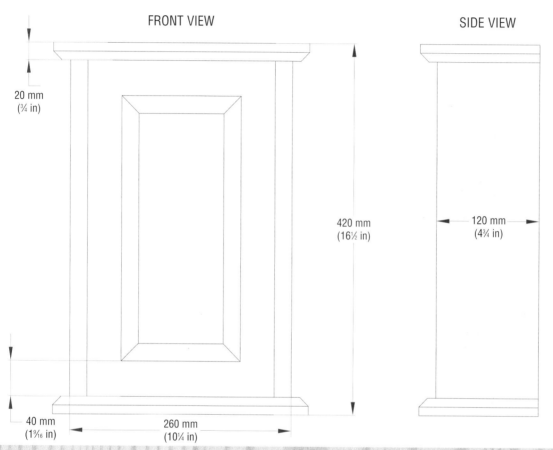

FRONT VIEW

SIDE VIEW

20 mm (¾ in)

420 mm (16½ in)

40 mm (1⁹⁄₁₆ in)

260 mm (10¼ in)

120 mm (4¾ in)

Essential tools
Measuring and marking tools
Crosscut and ripsaws
Biscuit jointer
Chisels
Bar clamps
G-clamps
Plane
Pin hammer
Bench vice

Router accessories
Router table
Straight cutter: 12.7 mm (½ in)
Bearing-guided chamfer cutter
Profile/ scriber cutter set
Panel-raising cutter

Cutting list
Top/ Base – 2 pieces ash, 300 x 140 x 20 mm (11¹³⁄₁₆ x 5½ x ¾ in)
Side – 2 pieces ash, 380 x 120 x 20 mm (15 x 4¾ x ¾ in)
Shelf – 1 piece ash, 225 x 90 x 12 mm (8⅞ x 3⁹⁄₁₆ x ½ in)
Back – 1 piece MDF, 400 x 235 x 6 mm (15¾ x 9¼ x ¼ in)

Door
Rail – 2 pieces ash, 155 x 40 x 20 mm (6⅛ x 1⁹⁄₁₆ x ¾ in)

Stile – 2 pieces ash, 380 x 40 x 20 mm (15 x 1⁹⁄₁₆ x ¾ in)
Panel – 1 piece rosewood, 315 x 150 x 15 mm (12⁷⁄₁₆ x 5¹⁵⁄₁₆ x ⁹⁄₁₆ in)

Additional materials
2 stop blocks
Battens: 2 battens, 150 x 40 x 20 mm (5¹⁵⁄₁₆ x 1⁹⁄₁₆ x ¾ in)
Glue
Abrasive paper
Hinges: 2 x 50-mm (2-in) solid brass butt hinges
Catch
Knob
Nails: 12-mm (½-in) panel pins

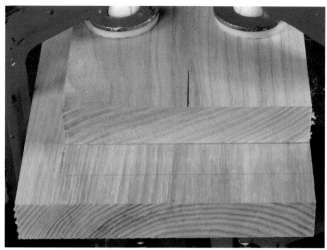

1 Cut the top, base and two sides to size. Mark the position of the sides on the top and base panels. They are set in 20 mm (¾ in) from the end, and it is important to mark the position of the inside face. Transfer the markings across both panels.

2 Mark the centre-point of each of the sides on the outside face, using the combination square. Make sure that the mark is clear as this is what you will use to position the biscuit jointer. Place one of the sides on the base panel with the inside edge lined up with the marked line. Use the G-clamps to clamp it in position with the rear edges lined up.

3 The joint is cut with a biscuit jointer, using the base of the tool as the reference. Make sure that the depth is set for size 20 biscuits. Stand the jointer vertically and place it hard against the end of the clamped side board. Cut a slot. Leaving the boards clamped together, use the biscuit jointer horizontally, lined up on the same mark, and cut a slot in the end of the side. Repeat this process for all four corners.

4 The next job is to cut the rebate to hold the back panel. This is simple to do on the sides. Fit the straight cutter in the router table and set the fence back so that the outside of the cutter is 6 mm (¼ in) away. Set the height of the cutter to around 10 mm (⅜ in). Mould the inside back edge of both sides.

5 Moulding the top and base panels is trickier, because the rebates do not run for the full length. Mark the exact position of the ends of the rebates by standing the sides in their correct position on the end panels. Put biscuits in the joints to locate them accurately. Mark the end of the rebate on the back of the base/top panel. Extend the line onto the underside/top of the panel.

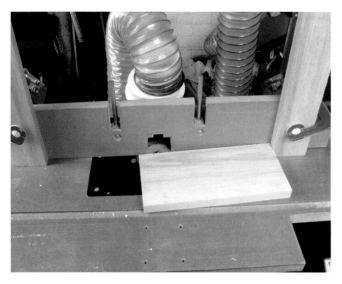

6 Place the panel on the router table with the cutter set as before. You need to limit the travel of the board so that you do not make the rebate too long. This is done by clamping stop blocks to the fence with the G-clamps. Set the panel on the table so that the front mark is just in front of the cutter. Clamp a block to the fence, hard up against the back of the board. Move the board forward and set it so that the rear mark is just behind the cutter. Now clamp another block to the fence, hard up against the front of the board.

7 To make the cut, start the router and hold the board at an angle against the rear stop block. Gently push it towards the cutter. As soon as it is flat against the fence, push it smoothly forward until it reaches the front stop block. Pull the rear of the board away from the cutter and turn off the router.

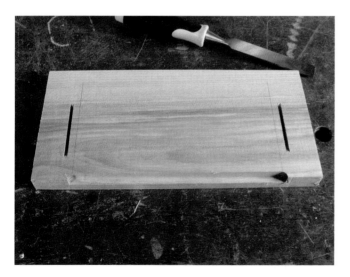

8 The completed rebate. Square off the ends of the rebate using a chisel.

9 Mould the inside faces of the top and base panels with the bearing-guided chamfer cutter. Set the fence in line with the cutter bearing and make a series of shallow passes, working around the board, starting on one end. Do not mould the back edge. After each pass, check the profile on the edge of the board. Keep raising the cutter for each pass until you are satisfied with the shape.

 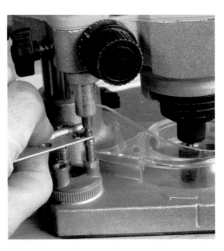 

10 It is a good idea to roughly assemble the cabinet to check it looks good. Before assembling the cabinet permanently, rout out the recesses for the hinges. Set the hinges 40 mm (1⁹⁄₁₆ in) in from the ends of the side panel. Mark their positions with a pencil. The hinge should be set into the board so that only half the knuckle protrudes.

11 To set the depth of cut, firstly fit the straight cutter. Stand the router on a flat board and, with the motor off, plunge the cutter down so that it just touches the board. Now take an open hinge and place it on top of the depth-setting turret. Wind down the depth adjuster until it touches the top of the hinge. Lock the depth stop, and when you plunge the router, it will go to exactly the right depth.

12 Carefully rout out the waste, being careful not to go over the lines. It is actually easier to plunge the router and lock it down, then start the motor and feed the cutter into the timber and move it along the edge between the marked lines. The side fence should be set to the width of the hinge leaf. Square off the ends of the completed recess with a chisel.

13 Next cut the housing for the internal shelf. This is a 'stopped' housing, which does not run the full width of the board. Mark out the position of the housing with a line across the centre of both side boards. Mark a point 25 mm (1 in) back from the front edge of each board. This is the place where the housing will end. Lay the two boards back to back on a workbench, and clamp a pair of battens across both boards in order to guide the router along the marked line. Make sure that the battens are parallel to each other and the marked line.

14 The router will sandwich itself neatly between the battens. The housing depth should be about 6 mm (¼ in). Be careful not to run over the end lines.

15 After routing the housings, square off the ends with a chisel. The cabinet frame is now ready to assemble. Do not try to fit the shelf now, but wait until the frame is complete. Apply glue to the biscuit joints and the board ends, and clamp up the assembly tightly with the bar clamps. Make sure that the cabinet is square and leave to dry.

16 Measure into the housings and cut the shelf to length. Plane it to the correct thickness, so that it slides into the frame. Apply a little glue to fix it in position. Cut the back panel to size and fit it into the rebate. Do not fix it in place yet, as you may want to remove it later to make it easier to fit the door catch.

17 To make the panelled door, you will need a dedicated profile/scriber cutter set. These cutters will mould the door frame, cut the joints and also mould the edge of the central panel.

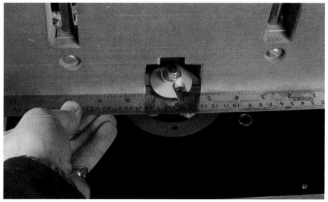

18 Before routing, the components must be cut to size. Measure the opening on the front of the cabinet and cut the two stiles (the uprights), so that they fit exactly. Place them in position and measure the space between them. The length of the rails (cross-pieces) should be this measurement plus an allowance for the length of the joints on their ends. First, cut the tenons on the end of the rails. Set the cutter to the correct height so that the tenon will be in the right position.

19 Set the fence exactly in line with the guide bearing on the cutter. Use a metal rule to ensure it is correct.

20 Moulding end-grain must be done with care, and because the rails on this door are particularly short, added precautions are necessary. To hold the rail at right angles to the cutter, use a wide board behind it. Press the ends of both boards up against the fence and clamp them together as shown in the picture. The rails are routed face up on the table. Repeat the process on both ends of each rail.

21 The cutter must now be reset to cut the profile and the groove on the inside edge of the door frame. On this cutter set, this is done simply by raising the cutter in the table. Place the rail face down on the table next to the cutter. Raise the cutter until the edge of the slotting cutter is exactly level with the tenon. This setting is critical to achieving a good joint.

22 The stiles and rails are moulded on their inside edges and are placed face down on the table. Again the shortness of the rails makes it difficult to mould them safely by hand, so take a piece of ply or MDF and cut out a section to hold the rail. Use this to run the rail safely past the cutter. The door frame should fit neatly together once all the routing has been done.

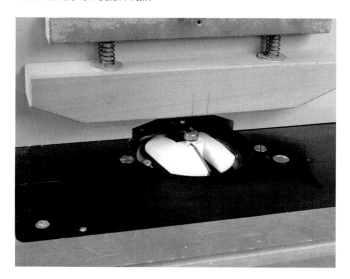 

23 Now the panel must be machined to fit the frame. Assemble the frame and measure the size into the grooves. Subtract 4 mm (³⁄₁₆ in) from the width and 2 mm (¹⁄₁₆ in) from the height and cut the panel to this size. A panel-raising cutter is used to cut the profile around the panel. This is a large-diameter cutter, which must be run at a slow speed – generally around 12,000 rpm.

24 Work around the panel, starting on the end-grain, and make shallow passes. Take time over this as it is important to produce a good finish. Raise the cutter a little after each pass. This obviously makes the edge thinner. Carry on until the panel is thin enough to slip into the groove in the door frame. It should be tight enough not to rattle, but not so tight that it jams.

25 Assemble the door dry (without glue) to test it, using bar clamps and making sure that all the joints fit snugly and the panel is secure. Dismantle, apply glue to the joints and reassemble. Be careful not to get any glue in the panel grooves – the panel must be free to move, otherwise it may split. Clamp up tightly and leave to dry.

26 The door will need a little adjustment before it fits the cabinet properly. Plane the sides evenly until it will fit the cabinet with a gap of approximately 1 mm (¹⁄₃₂ in) on all sides.

27 Fit the hinges in the cabinet and fix with one screw each. Open the hinges and stand the door in position in the cabinet. Fold a piece of abrasive paper and place it under the corner of the door to lift it off the base panel. Fold the hinges over the front of the door and mark their position with a pencil.

28 Fit the door into the bench vice and transfer the pencil marks on to the back edge. Rout out the hinge recesses using exactly the same settings used on the cabinet side. Be very careful to hold the router level on the door edge, because there is not a great deal of support and it is easy to let it tip. Square off the ends of the recesses after routing. Temporarily fit the door with one screw per hinge and check the fit. Remove and make any necessary adjustments. When you are happy with the fit and the door shows an even gap on all sides, carefully fit all the screws and tighten. Fit a knob and a catch to hold the door shut. Finally, fix the back in place with hammer and panel pins.

Coffee table

Living rooms are not as large as they used to be, so any furniture needs to earn its keep. This design for a small coffee table also features convenient and unusual storage space: the top panels slide open to give access to the space below. The panels are made from a contrasting timber and slide in grooves cut into the top boards. Beech has been used for the main frame and American cherry for the sliding panels.

Essential tools
Measuring and marking tools
F- or G-clamp
Tenon saw, rip saw and coping saw or jigsaw
Plane and orbital sander
Bar clamps
Biscuit jointer
Pocket hole jig
Screwdriver and chisels

Router accessories
Router table
Slotting cutter: 4 mm (³⁄₁₆ in)

Straight cutters: 9 mm (⅜ in) and 18 mm (¹¹⁄₁₆ in)

Cutting list
Legs – 4 pieces beech, 280 x 70 x 35 mm (11³⁄₁₆ x 2¾ x 1⅜ in)
Side rails – 2 pieces beech, 620 x 120 x 20 mm (24⁷⁄₁₆ x 4¾ x ¾ in)
End rails – 2 pieces beech, 390 x 120 x 20 mm (15⅜ x 4¾ x ¾ in)
Centre rail – 1 piece beech, 275 x 150 x 20 mm (10¹³⁄₁₆ x 5¹⁵⁄₁₆ x ¾ in)
Top board – 2 pieces beech, 800 x 120 x 20 mm (31⁷⁄₁₆ x 4¾ x ¾ in)

Centre board – 1 piece beech, 275 x 150 x 20 mm (10¹³⁄₁₆ x 5¹⁵⁄₁₆ x ¾ in)
Sliding panels – 2 pieces cherry, 280 x 360 x 20 mm (11³⁄₁₆ x 14³⁄₁₆ x ¾ in)
Base panel – 1 piece MDF, 680 x 380 x 6 mm (26¾ x 15 x ¼ in)

Additional materials
Glue
Abrasive paper
Screws: 16 x 4 mm x 25 mm (³⁄₁₆ x 1 in)

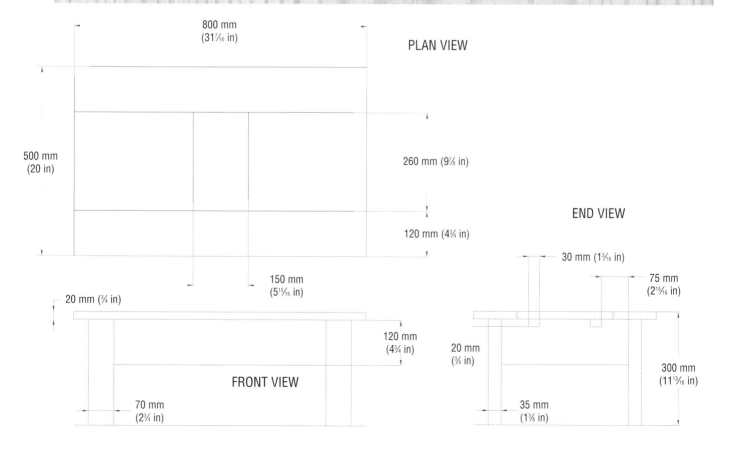

PLAN VIEW

800 mm
(31⁷⁄₁₆ in)

500 mm
(20 in)

260 mm (9⅞ in)

120 mm (4¾ in)

END VIEW

30 mm (1³⁄₁₆ in)

75 mm
(2¹⁵⁄₁₆ in)

20 mm (¾ in)

150 mm
(5¹⁵⁄₁₆ in)

120 mm
(4¾ in)

FRONT VIEW

70 mm
(2¾ in)

20 mm
(¾ in)

35 mm
(1⅜ in)

300 mm
(11¹³⁄₁₆ in)

1 Cut the frame components to size (four legs, two side rails and two end rails). The mortises must then be marked out. Lay one rail on top of a leg, making sure that the top of the leg is flush with the top of the board. Check that it is square and then mark the width of the rail on the leg. Extend the line onto the edge of the leg. Stand the leg on its edge and find the centre-line. Mark this and then mark another horizontal line 10 mm (⅜ in) down from the top. The mortise will be cut directly on the centre-line and between the two marked horizontal lines.

2 One difficulty with cutting mortises near to the end of components is that there is little support for the router and so it can topple off. The simplest way to prevent this is to clamp two legs end to end on the bench, and then cut the joints so that as the router runs off the top of one leg it is still supported by the end of the other leg.

3 Cut the joint: line up the cutter on the centre-line and lock the side fence. Use the 9 mm (⅜ in) cutter and set the depth of cut to just over 20 mm (¾ in). Cut the joint in a series of passes, making sure that you do not go over the horizontal lines. Repeat this on both faces of each leg, using the same fence setting (so that both mortises are the same distance from the outside edge). The router will obviously cut a round-ended mortise. You can either make a round-ended tenon to fit it or square off the ends of the mortise with a chisel.

4 The tenons are cut on the router table. Mark the length of the tenon, 20 mm (¾ in), on the end of the rail. Fit the larger straight cutter into the router table. Now set the fence so that the cutter will just reach the marked line. To achieve the correct tenon thickness, make a shallow pass on each side and then check the fit in the mortise. Repeat the process, making passes equally on both sides until the tenon is a snug fit in the mortise. At this stage it will be too long. Trim off the top 10 mm (⅜ in) of the tenon with a tenon saw to match the mortise.

5 Because the frame of the table also provides the storage space, a bottom panel will be fitted once the rest of the table is complete. However, you need to cut the rebate for it before the frame is assembled. Again, do this on the router table using a straight cutter. Set the height of the cutter so that it reaches about halfway into the thickness of the side rail, and fence so that the width of the rebate is about 7 mm (¼ in). Machine all four sides of the completed rebate.

6 The sliding panels will have supporting bars fixed to their underside to hold them flat. The end rails must have cut-outs to accommodate these. Refer to the drawing, mark out, and make a series of vertical sawcuts using a tenon saw or pullsaw. Remove the waste with a coping saw and then clean up the base of the recess with a chisel.

7 Before assembling the frame, sand all the components with an orbital sander. Glue the frame together in two stages. First take the long rails and glue the legs onto each end. Apply glue to the mortise rather than the tenon, as it will then be pushed into the joint when the tenon is inserted. Use a bar clamp to hold the assembly together tightly while the glue cures.

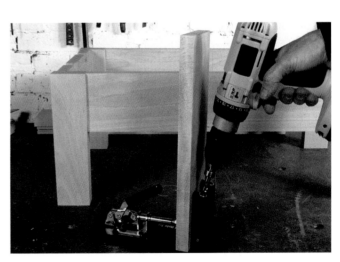

8 Next, glue the shorter rails in place. Again use the bar clamps and make sure that the whole frame is exactly square by measuring the diagonals with a rule. They must be identical. If they are not, remove the clamps and straighten the frame, before reapplying the clamps. Make sure that the frame is standing on a perfectly level surface and that all the legs are stable.

9 Fit the central rail when the frame is complete. Measure the frame and cut the rail so that it is a sliding fit in the frame. To hold it in position, use a pocket hole jig and bore through both ends. Before installing the rail, use the pocket hole jig to make a series of holes along the top edge, in order to fix the top down. Do the same on the main frame side rails.

10 Make up the top boards. Start by preparing the two side boards. Cut the boards to length and set up the router table to machine the groove that the panels will slide along. It should be 8 mm (⁵⁄₁₆ in) wide and 5 mm (³⁄₁₆ in) deep. Use a 4-mm (³⁄₁₆-in) slotting cutter and make two passes, turning the board over in between. This ensures that the groove will be centrally positioned in the thickness of the board.

11 When you have completed the groove, place the boards in position on the frame and measure the precise length of the central board. You must measure into the bottom of the groove. Cut the board to this length and then groove the sides to match the side boards.

12 Now cut a matching tenon on both ends of the central board. Using an 18-mm (¹¹⁄₁₆-in) straight cutter, make a shallow pass on each side of the board and then check the fit in the groove. Repeat this until the tenon is a snug fit in the groove.

13 Fix the jointed boards to the frame. It is important that the outside boards are exactly parallel, otherwise the sliding panels will not move smoothly. Position the boards on the frame – use a dab of glue in the centre of the tenon on the centre board, but do not glue its full width as it needs to be free to move. Clamp the boards in place, turn the table over and screw through the pocket holes.

14 To make up the sliding panels, you will need to joint together several boards edge to edge. When the panels are installed, the grain must run parallel to the centre board, otherwise there is a risk of them expanding and jamming in their grooves. The boards must be prepared to the same thickness as the rest of the top. Strengthen the joints with a biscuit jointer.

15 The panels must be a precise fit in the grooves, so measure carefully before cutting them to size. Cut the tongues on three sides of the panels using the same technique as for making the tenons on the centre board. Keep checking the fit after each pass, and make sure that you do not make them too thin. The panel should move smoothly within the groove, with an even gap on all sides. When satisfied with the fit, trim to length.

16 Because the width of the sliding panels is unsupported, they need to have bearer bars fixed to their undersides to hold them flat. These are attached with three screws each. The central screw is bored and countersunk as normal; however the outer two holes must be enlarged along the length of the bearer to allow for any movement in the boards. Screw the bearers in place with the panels in position, and make sure that they line up with the cut-outs in the end rails.

17 Finally, take a short offcut and fix it to the end of each panel to stop it falling out of the table each time the panels are opened.

18 Once the panels have been fitted and are operating smoothly, the base panel can be fitted. Measure the rebate and cut the panel to size. A tenon saw can be used to remove the corners to accommodate the legs. Screw the panel in place, so that it can be removed should there be any problems with the panels in the future.

Suppliers and useful addresses

UNITED KINGDOM

General DIY Stores

B & Q plc (outlets nationwide)
Head Office:
Portswood House
1 Hampshire Corporate Park
Chandlers Ford, Eastleigh
Hampshire SO53 3YX
Tel: 0845 609 6688
www.diy.com

Focus DIY Ltd (outlets nationwide)
Head Office:
Gawsworth House
Westmere Drive
Crewe
Cheshire CW1 6XB
Tel: 01270 501 555
www.focusdiy.co.uk

Homebase Ltd (outlets nationwide)
Head Office:
Beddington House
Railway Approach
Wallington
Surrey SM6 0HB
Tel: 020 8784 7200
www.homebase.co.uk

Hardwood Retailers and Timberyards

North Heigham Sawmills Ltd
26 Paddock Street
Norwich
Norfolk NR2 4TW
Tel: 01603 622 978

South London Hardwoods
390 Sydenham Road
Croydon
Surrey CR0 2EA
Tel: 020 8683 0292

Ironmongery

Isaac Lord
185 Desborough Road
High Wycombe
Buckinghamshire HP11 2QN
Tel: 01494 462 121

Router Tables and Accessories

Trend Machinery & Cutting Tools Ltd
Unit 6 St Alban's Road
Odhams Trading Estate
Watford
Hertfordshire WD24 7TR
Tel: 01923 221 910/249 911

Tool Manufacturers

Black & Decker
210 Bath Road
Slough
Berkshire SL1 3YD
Tel: 01753 511 234
www.blackanddecker.co.uk

Stanley UK Holdings Ltd
Sheffield Business Park
Sheffield City Airport
Europa Link
Sheffield
Yorkshire S3 9PD
Tel: 0114 276 8888
www.stanleyworks.com

Tool Retailers

S. J. Carter Tools Ltd
74 Elmers End Road
London SE20 7UX
Tel: 020 8659 7222

Tilgear
Bridge House
69 Station Road
Cuffley, Potters Bar
Hertfordshire EN6 4TG
Tel: 01707 873 434

The following woodworking magazines can also provide a national overview of woodworking retailers:

Furniture & Cabinet Making

The Guild of Master Craftsmen
166 High Street
Lewes
East Sussex
BN7 1XU
Tel: 01273 488 005
www.thegmcgroup.com

Practical Woodworking and The Woodworker

Berwick House
8-10 Knoll Rise
Orpington
Kent
BR6 0EL
Tel: 01689 899 200
www.getwoodworking.com

Traditional Woodworking

The Well House
High Street
Burton-on-Trent
Staffordshire
DE14 1JQ
Tel: 01283 742 950

SOUTH AFRICA

Hardware and DIY Retailers

Mica (outlets nationwide)
Tel: 031 573 2442
www.mica.co.za

Wardkiss Paint and Hardware Centre
329 Sydney Road
Durban 4001
Tel: 031 205 1551

Timber Retailers

Citiwood
339 Main Reef Road
Denver 2094 (Johannesburg)
Tel: 011 622 9360

Coleman Timbers
Unit 3, Willowfield Crescent
Springfield Park Industria 4091 (Durban)
Tel: 031 579 1565

Federated Timbers
17 McKenzie Street
Industrial Sites
Bloemfontein 9301
Tel: 051 447 3171

Penny Pinchers
261 Lansdowne Road
Claremont 7780 (Cape Town)
Tel: 021 683 0380

Timber City
74 5th Avenue
Newton Park 6045 (Port Elizabeth)
Tel: 041 365 3586

Tool Retailers

J & J Sales
38 Argyle Street
East London 5201
Tel: 043 743 3380

Tooltrick
55A Bok Street
Pietersburg 0700
Tel: 015 295 5982

AUSTRALIA

General DIY Stores

Carroll's Woodcraft Supplies
66 Murradoc Road
Drysdale
Vic 3222
Tel: 03 5251 3874
www.cws.au.com

Hardware

Boxmakers Brassware
PO Box 136 Dungog
NSW 2420
Tel 02 4992 3068
www.boxmakersbrassware.com.au

Mother of Pearl & Sons Trading
Rushcutters Bay
34-36 McLachlan Avenue
NSW 2011
Tel: 02 9332 4455

Timber Suppliers

Trend Timbers
Lot 1
Cunneen Street
Mulgrave/McGrath's Hill
NSW 2756
Tel: 02 4577 5277
www.trendtimbers.com.au

Tool Retailers

Carba-Tec Pty Ltd (outlets nationwide)
Head Office:
40 Harries Road
Coorparoo
QLD 4151
Tel: 07 3397 2577
www.carbatec.com.au
Colen Clenton
20 Long Street
Cessnock 2325
Tel 02 4990 7956

Hare & Forbes Machinery House
(outlets nationwide)
Head Office:
The Junction
2 Windsor Road
Northmead
NSW 2152
Tel: 02 9890 9111
www.hareandforbes.com.au

**H. N. T. Gordon & Co Classic Plane
Makers**
50 Northcott Crescent
Alstonville
NSW 2477
Tel: 612 6628 7222
www.hntgordon.com.au

Timbecon Pty Ltd
10-12 John Street
Bentley
WA 6102
Tel: 08 9356 1653
www.timbecon.com.au

The Wood Works Book & Tool Co
8 Railway Road
Meadowbank
NSW 2114
Tel 02 9807 7244
www.thewoodworks.com.au

NEW ZEALAND

General DIY Stores

Bunnings Warehouse
(outlets nationwide)
www.bunnings.co.nz

Hammer Hardware (outlets nationwide)
Private Bag 102925
North Shore Mail Centre
Auckland 1330
Tel: 09 443 9953
www.hammerhardware.co.nz

**Mitre 10 (New Zealand) Ltd (outlets
nationwide)**
Private Bag 102925
North Shore Mail Centre
Auckland
Tel: 09 443 9900
www.mitre10.co.nz

PlaceMakers (outlets nationwide)
Support Office:
15- Marua Road
Ellerslie
Auckland
Tel: 09 525 5100
www.placemakers.co.nz

Index